Lost Restaurants

OF

KNOXVILLE

Lost Restaurants

OF

KNOXVILLE

PAULA A. JOHNSON

Foreword by Grady Regas

AMERICAN PALATE

Published by American Palate
A Division of The History Press
Charleston, SC
www.historypress.net

Cover image, top left: Peter Kern Building. *The McClung Collection*; *top middle*: Patrick Sullivan's Saloon. *Library of Congress*; *top right*: S&W Cafeteria. *The McClung Collection*; *bottom*: The Inferno. *The Tichnor Brothers Collection.*
Back cover, bottom: Kress Lunch Counter. *The McClung Collection*; *top*: Harold's Kosher Food Center. *The McClung Collection.*

First published 2017

ISBN 9781540227522

Library of Congress Control Number: 2017948483

This book is dedicated…to everyone who lived their dream.

CONTENTS

Contents

FOREWORD

Wow-wee! *Lost Restaurants* is an amazing, thrilling ride through Knoxville's hospitality history. Paula Johnson needs to be celebrated for completing what must have felt like an endurance test, the research required to write this book covering such a deliciously generous portion of Knoxville's 227-year food service and hospitality history.

There is value in finding what has been lost. Paula's research helps to discover things about Knoxville restaurants and simultaneously uncovers and reconnects us to our history that may have otherwise remained lost. I believe you can really only learn what you almost already know. Although I have spent my life on the periphery of hearsay history and hospitality stories, this book helped me to learn that hearsay is not a very reliable source of history. I am grateful to Paula for taking on such a huge topic as reviewing the highlights of Knoxville's restaurants over the last twenty-two and a half decades. These restaurants were born into our community, danced around with the diverse culinary and hospitality curiosity and insatiable appetites of our fellow Knoxvillians and visitors for a time and have since been relegated to a collection of tasty memories.

I enjoyed the first-person presentation style Paula chose for this book. Not only did she share historic facts that she found in numerous sources, but she also shared with us the added color she experienced from her business, Knoxville Food Tours. I am looking forward now to taking her tour very soon.

I shared the working draft of *Lost Restaurants* with my dad, Bill Regas, who was born in 1929 in Knoxville. He has invested all of his professional life, aside from his experience at Tennessee Military Institute and his service in the U.S. Army, in the wonderful world of hospitality in Knoxville. He also learned a great deal from *Lost Restaurants* and found the book hard to put down.

Today is the ninety-eighth anniversary of Regas Restaurant's founding. As a third-generation Regas family member who has been around the legendary, historic stories of our family's business history as well as stories of restaurants, restaurant entrepreneurs and hospitality team members, I found *Lost Restaurants* to be quite enlightening. For example, I learned in chapter 7 that in 1875, the Schubert Hotel served a "Tennessee delicacy" of opossum with a milk puree of sweet potatoes. I also learned in chapter 13 that the S&W Cafeteria on Gay Street served up to seven hundred customers per hour. Wow! That's amazing!

I really appreciated that Paula dedicated *Lost Restaurants* "to *everyone* who lived their dream." The number of people in the hospitality industry whom "*everyone*" includes is unknown and unknowable. I learned in chapter 13 that the S&W Cafeteria required a staff of 250 people in order to operate on all cylinders. I wonder how many people were employed just at S&W over fifty-two years. Each of these staff members had a dream to pursue. Each of them had a story. I loved hearing about S&W server Tennyson "Slim" Dickson. I remember my mother, Elizabeth Frost Regas, introducing me to Slim and recall how nice he was to me. Each restaurant team member made individual contributions to the momentum of the restaurant and perhaps even to the ultimate fate of the restaurant of which they were a part. Most of those contributions were positive, while others may have proved injurious to the establishment. Perhaps in their own little way, some staff members contributed to the demise of their particular restaurant, adding yet another establishment to the list of lost restaurants. That part of restaurant history remains a mystery and the product of twisted hearsay passed around and around. I have learned again through this book that not all hospitality dreams are sweet; some become nightmares. Today, there are 1,400-plus restaurants in Knox County composed of the joyous dreams of hospitality entrepreneurs and team members alike, many inspired directly or indirectly by hospitality professions mentioned in *Lost Restaurants*. By taking advantage of Knoxville's hospitality history lessons in *Lost Restaurants*, there is time to learn and still room to chase the sweet American dream by sharing delicious tastes and fond memories.

Thank you for helping us learn, Paula. Nice work!

—Grady Regas

ACKNOWLEDGEMENTS

A special thank-you to my parents for their love, support and encouragement.

Additional thanks to Jannelle Jones, Jenni Schaming, Harrison Schaming, Margaret Manley, Crystal Huskey, Jack Flinchem, Martha Boggs, Rex Jones, Flo Ullrich, Madeline Hassil, Peter Ullrich, Grady Regas, Jenny Williams, Bill Regas, Susan Witt, Mahasti Vafaie, Scott Partin, Frank Sparkman, Wesley Morgan, Steve Cotham and Eric Dawson.

INTRODUCTION

Knoxville, Tennessee, is a city unlike any other—with a respect for its historic beginnings and old mountain ways mixed with new and modern business and trends. Rich farmland begins not far outside town and has produced nationally known food brands Bush's Beans and Mayfield Dairy, as well as renowned chef favorites Benton's Smoky Ham and Bacon and Cruze Dairy Farm. White Lily Flour and JFG Coffee both operated in Knoxville for over one hundred years.

Energy is a major focus in the city, with the proximity to the Oak Ridge National Laboratory and the nation's largest power provider, the Tennessee Valley Authority. The entertainment industry plays a major role as well, with Scripps Networks and the Regal Entertainment Group both headquartered here. Knoxville is close to the tourist destination of the Great Smoky Mountains National Park, which is the most visited national park in the United States, as well as Blackberry Farm, one of this country's most lauded luxury resorts. Students from all fifty states and over one hundred foreign countries come to study at the University of Tennessee, which reaches enrollment of over twenty-five thousand.

Knoxville has the distinction of having one of the highest numbers of restaurants per capita in the nation, and our central geographic location and steady economy contribute to an often-used test market for new restaurant concepts and food products. There are thousands of "lost restaurants" of Knoxville. Here I've gathered a collection of highlights for your enjoyment and for your acclimation to our fair city.

Welcome to Knoxville. Sit and visit with us for a spell.

PART I

Knoxville's Early Days: Taming a Frontier

CHAPTER 1

CHISHOLM'S TAVERN

KNOXVILLE'S FIRST EATING AND DRINKING ESTABLISHMENT

Here in Knoxville, we are famous for our history and our preservation of history. The commitment to this preservation began to appear in the 1930s, when various groups of enthusiastic Knoxvillians took a notion to save John Chisholm's Tavern, Knoxville's first eating and drinking establishment.

John Chisholm was known as a hearty Scot and described as robust, red-haired, red-faced, brawny, weather-beaten, quick-tempered, generous and a loyal Patriot. He is said to have loved a tall tale and a good fight and was once fined for beating up a man for being an active Tory.

Chisholm left Scotland after the "Jacobite Upheaval" in 1745. He traveled first to South Carolina, then to Virginia and finally settled in the Watauga-Nolachucky, or "Washington District," region of North Carolina in the early 1770s. His influence helped to shape the early policies of the Watauga Association, where he served as a justice for many years. He also worked as a surveyor under James Stuart to lay off the tracts granted by the federal government to soldiers for their service in the Revolutionary War and those purchased by early settlers from the Indians. In 1784, he became a delegate, along with John Sevier, to the convention held in Greeneville to establish the ill-fated and short-lived state of Franklin, a predecessor of the state of Tennessee.

Chisholm arrived in what is now Knoxville, at James White's Fort, in 1790, with William Blount. Blount had been a signer of the U.S. Constitution and was sent to the area by George Washington to govern the new Southwest Territory, or the territory south of the Ohio River. He was a skilled negotiator and was successful with his task of forming the Holston Treaty with the Cherokee Indians. Following their arrival at the fort, Chisholm and Blount each bought one of the half-acre lots offered for sale by James White overlooking the Tennessee River, where Chisholm established the area's first tavern.

James White settled in this area in the late 1780s, following his service in the Revolutionary War. The two-story log fort he built was selected as the capital of the Southwest Territory. In 1791, White hired his son-in-law, Charles McClung, to survey and divide a portion of his land for the establishment of a church and to form Blount College, later to be known as the University of Tennessee. Sixty-four half-acre lots were also set aside to create a town to be called Knoxville, in honor of Henry Knox, President Washington's secretary of war and the direct supervisor of William Blount at that time. The lots were offered for sale by lottery at eight dollars each.

With the opening of his tavern, John Chisholm became Knoxville's first entrepreneur, and his wife, Patsy, who handled the majority of activity of the establishment, is known as Knoxville's first businesswoman. Patsy was acknowledged as an excellent manager and also offered tailoring service to the settlers and Indians. The tavern building was described as having a bar in one corner of the great room, but the dining room and kitchen were separated from the main building by a narrow passageway. Breakfast was offered at twenty cents, dinner (lunch) at twenty-five cents and supper at sixteen and two-thirds cents. If a patron received a meal of "cold victuals," it was at one-half price, taking into consideration the value of stove wood. Whiskey was offered at eighty cents for one half pint. The majority of guests at the tavern rode horseback, and the price of corn for horses was fixed at ten cents a gallon or eighty cents a bushel. A room for the night was six cents.

Chisholm also ran a side business of a beef market, where, as listed in the *Knoxville Gazette* of 1792, he offered "Fresh Meat, 3 Days a Week—Cash." In addition to being well stocked with beef, the tavern most likely kept another of Chisholm's favorites on hand, as he, by his own confession, liked a stiff drink of taffa rum. Taffa, taffia or tafia is made from a low-grade sugar cane juice. Rum is typically made by an aging process, but taffa was an unaged variant. You might already be familiar with the East Tennessean penchant for the kick of an unaged spirit. Rum and taffa date back to the time of the vast sugar cane plantations of the West Indies in the seventeenth century. In the colonial era, rum was associated with the trade routes and became a very lucrative business.

Although there are no culinary records left from Chisholm's Tavern, according to eighteenth-century cooking scholars, pork was the most popular meat of the time. Meals at the tavern might have also included venison, beef, turkey, chicken, partridge and various birds, mussels, oysters, fish and eggs. Stew was often made with the available meats and vegetables. Commonly grown vegetables were turnips, white and sweet potatoes, cabbage, beans, peas and peppers. Asparagus was used as a dish on its own and also as a garnish. An interesting dish of the time was sweet potatoes mashed with an egg, formed into balls, dipped in butter and bread crumbs and browned in a Dutch oven. Herbs from herb gardens were used in daily cooking, as were nasturtiums, which provided a bit of spice as well as a beautiful presentation. Milk, butter, flour, cornmeal, cinnamon and nutmeg were available by 1750. Citrus fruits such as lemons and oranges would arrive by wagon from the coast and would often not be in the freshest condition upon arrival but could be used in cooking. Table centerpieces were created from fruits and nuts. After meals, women would customarily leave the table so that the men could talk business and politics and continue to snack on fruits, nuts and cheeses, which might be baked on stale bread until the cheese puffed. Hospitality traditions of the time dictated the choicest morsels would go to visitors.

Beyond the tavern, the ever-enterprising John Chisholm also established a postal route to Jefferson and Greene Counties, Jonesboro and through to Abingdon, Virginia. This early post route is considered by some as Chisholm's greatest achievement of public service, making him the forerunner of the rural free delivery of mail.

John Chisholm's intriguing legacy doesn't end there. The famous trail for the great cattle drives, the Chisholm Trail, was originally scouted and marked by his grandson Jesse Chisholm.

Chisholm's Tavern hosted many distinguished visitors. A letter from William Blount in 1795 to the federal government's Indian agent, Colonel David Henley, noted that a number of the principal Cherokee Indian chiefs from the nearby Tellico Plains area desired to visit Knoxville. The chiefs reasoned that it would be an opportunity for their young warriors to witness that there was peace not only with this newly established government but also with the settlers at large. Blount relates that he verbally directed the Cherokee to Mrs. Chisholm's house, where, as there was an understanding with Mrs. Chisholm, they would be well treated. Blount communicated that Chisholm's Tavern was the most proper house in town to entertain the Indian chiefs and, "I may add, the only proper one."

Other notable visitors to Chisholm's Tavern included Andrew Jackson, who frequently passed through while traveling to serve as the first representative of the new state of Tennessee and as United States senator. Jackson also rode circuit over the state while serving as judge of the Tennessee Supreme Court and visited Knoxville often during that time.

Lafayette, the French aristocrat and military officer who became a close personal friend of George Washington during the Revolutionary War, was also a known guest at Chisholm's.

The Duke of Orleans, Louis Philippe, who later became king of France, once spent the night at the tavern while on a tour of the United States with his two brothers. Years later, as an American was presented at the Court of Versailles, Louis Philippe, perhaps fondly remembering his tour of the American wilds, inquired, chuckling, "Do they still sleep three to a bed in Tennessee?"

Over the years, the building on Front Street deteriorated and was slated for demolition. A valiant effort to save Chisholm's Tavern was mounted by Knoxville residents. Letters and articles were written and published in the newspaper, money was raised and associations were formed specifically to save the tavern, with the desire to combine the property with Blount Mansion

The colonial home thought to be Chisholm's Tavern. *Library of Congress.*

to create a historic park to encourage tourism and to give schoolchildren an opportunity to learn more about the city's founding fathers. The Daughters of the American Revolution, the Blount Mansion Association, the Sons of the Revolution, the East Tennessee Historical Society, Church Street United Methodist Church, the Chisholm Tavern Association, a group from the U.S. Marines and the Blount Memorial Park Association were all involved with the effort to save the building on James White's Lot 32, noting it their obligation, responsibility, privilege and duty. Then a predicament was brought to light: John Chisholm bought White's Lot 17, not Lot 32. The records were found by Pollyanna Creekmore, and the report was corroborated by civil engineer James S. Bowman.

The Creekmore/Bowman report showed that Lot 32 was originally drawn by a Matthew A. Atkinson, who must have declined the offer, for the first deed on record is from James White to Joseph Baker in 1792, for twelve dollars. In 1807, Joseph Baker deeded the land to John N. Gamble for twenty dollars.

Noted architect Charles Barber had this response to the report: "So it is not the original Chisholm Tavern, eh? So what! The mantels and other woodwork in this old building are as fine as any you'll find in any Colonial mansions in New England, Virginia, Charleston, or New Orleans. It is period architecture of the best type and it all deserves to be preserved and prized."

The fate of Chisholm's Tavern is not known, but once it was proven that the building on Lot 32 was not the original tavern, the restoration effort was put aside. The house was razed in 1966 to create Neyland Drive.

CHAPTER 2

ARCHIE RHEA'S, AMERICAN CHOP SUEY AND THE LEGACY OF MARGARET HUMES

The name Archie Rhea's Tavern may not be well known to many, but it was the first commercial business in the building that most everyone familiar with Knoxville now knows as the Bijou. The original section of the building was begun in 1815 by Knoxville merchant Thomas Humes, who, unfortunately, passed away while it was being built.

Thomas Humes was born in Ireland in 1767 but immigrated to the American colonies as a child. He settled in Knoxville around 1795. Humes bought part of James White's Lot 38 of the original division of the city in 1801 and began establishing himself as a merchant. Humes has been described as a man "universally loved and trusted for his strict probity and kindly, benevolent disposition."

Humes opened a store on his property on Gay Street and did a thriving business in Knoxville, where little manufacturing existed at the time but where trade was reported to be brisker and shops better stocked than in Nashville. In 1805, he bought additional land in Lot 38 with plans to build. Humes had married Margaret Russell Cowan, and they, with their five children, were living in his store building. There was a delay with the construction, and Humes never had the opportunity to see the building completed. He suffered from an infection and died on September 23, 1816.

Thomas Humes died with a total of cash on hand of over $20,000 and outstanding accounts owed to him at nearly $50,000. Although Humes died a wealthy man, leaving his family in a comfortable situation, you've already heard about those East Tennessee businesswomen. The savvy Margaret

Humes was able to continue with the construction of the new building, and although it may have originally been intended as a private residence for the Humes family, she insisted that it was built specifically with the purpose to be used as a tavern. Her persistence paid off when she was able to obtain a lease with Archibald Rhea, the son-in-law of John Sevier, to move his tavern from Market Street to the new space.

The Humes building was considered a modern and even pretentious structure at the time of its completion and contained all the conveniences available in the best hotels in the country. The building was designed in the prevailing Georgian style—a three-story building with a basement or cellar, with a central hall running through it and rooms on each side. Basements were important features in buildings of frontier towns for the storage of supplies coming in.

Years later, the city completed a public works project on Gay Street. The north end of Gay Street was raised from the train depot by use of viaducts, and this south end of Gay Street was lowered, making the main road in hilly Knoxville more even and easy for travel. This heavy grading of Gay Street converted the basement of the Humes building into a ground floor, as we know it now. The bricks used for the building were molded by hand at a brickyard in what we now know as the Bearden District. They were hauled to the site on Gay Street on wagons drawn by oxen. On the southern façade, there was a second-story veranda that faced a large open space, or the inn yard, where stagecoaches could drive in from the road.

An ad run by Margaret Humes provides further description of the building:

> *The house is much larger than any other in East Tennessee, is in the centre of business, and well constructed for a TAVERN for which purpose it was built. The building contains thirteen spacious ROOMS besides the BAR ROOM, in each of which is a Fire place. The BALL ROOM and DINING ROOM are both very large and each have two fire places. Attached to the House are two commodious STABLES, an OUT LOT, GRAINARY, TWO KITCHENS and every other necessary building. Suffice it to say, that taken altogether, it is as well calculated for business as any in the western country will always command the principal business in the place, and cannot fail, if judiciously conducted, of realizing a profit to the tenant.*

Archie Rhea's Tavern and the Knoxville Hotel opened in the space in 1817. In his advertisements, Rhea assured those planning to patronize the tavern that his attention would be particularly devoted to render their situation easy and comfortable. Elegant rooms would be supplied with some of the day's most respectable newspapers for his guests' perusal.

Rhea's Tavern quickly became the center of Knoxville's social life. In addition to the bar and dining offerings, the building also hosted many other social gatherings. A school of dancing was opened in the facility, and a "practice ball" was held every other Friday at six o'clock in the evening in Mr. Rhea's Ballroom.

The grandest celebration held at Archie Rhea's Tavern was for Andrew Jackson in March 1819. News of Jackson's impending arrival had reached Knoxville, and a delegation specifically appointed for the purpose was assembled to meet him on the road. An elegant dinner for upward of 120 men was prepared by Mrs. Rhea for the occasion, and festivities continued until midnight.

By 1821, Margaret Humes was advertising the building again for rent. The building then passed through many different hands and operated under different business names. The name that lingered the longest was the Lamar House Hotel. It was suggested to the then proprietor, Sampson Lanier, that the name Lamar be used in honor of Gazaway Bugg Lamar, who showed a financial interest in Knoxville in the 1850s. He purchased Knoxville municipal bonds, most likely issued to finance the railroad development. He also, along with several other New York investors, was responsible for building a suburb north of the East Tennessee and Virginia Railroad tracks. Lamar had established himself in factories, shipping, insurance and warehousing. During the Civil War, he was active in supporting the efforts of the Confederacy by founding the Importing and Exporting Company of Georgia, which was one of the blockade runners of the war. He dealt extensively in guano (a type of fertilizer), cotton and tobacco.

The Humes building survived the ravages of the Civil War by its occupation as a hospital, first by the Confederacy and later by the Union. The most well-known name associated with the hospital was that of Union general William P. Sanders. Sanders had a bit of a rough start in his military career. His letter of dismissal from West Point was written by the then superintendent of the academy, Robert E. Lee, based on Sanders's accumulation of demerits, his deficiency in academics and his general want of application. Sanders managed to stay on and graduate from West

Point by some help from United States secretary of war Jefferson Davis, who happened to be Sanders's cousin.

Sanders's initiative and bravery became apparent during the war, as the Kentucky-born and Mississippi-raised man with Southern leanings fought for the preservation of the Union. In 1863, General Ambrose Burnside chose Sanders to lead a raid into East Tennessee, urged by President Lincoln, who considered the area both politically and militarily important. It is noted that in this area of the country, one of the great tragedies of the Civil War was that it was often brother against brother, which was the case for the Sanders family. During picket duty along the Tennessee River, Sanders made a request to headquarters to see if he might be allowed to write a letter to his brother, who was serving in the Confederacy, and leave it where the Rebel cavalry might find it and forward it on.

Burnside had given Sanders the orders to hold off incoming Confederates while fortifications were dug around Knoxville. While making their stand about a mile from the entrenchments, on a high hill on Kingston Road, Sanders was wounded by a sharpshooter and taken to the hospital at the Lamar House, where he later died. In yet another tragedy of the war, the Confederates were under the command at the time of Colonel Edward Porter Alexander, who had been Sanders's classmate and roommate at West Point. Sanders was buried at night, under the cover of darkness, to keep the news from demoralizing his troops.

Generals William Sherman and Philip Sheridan reportedly laid out battle plans on the dining room table of the Lamar House. General Sherman provided some insight into the food of Knoxville during the war, writing that, arriving in Knoxville and crossing the river by pontoon, they saw a large pen with a fine lot of cattle. Sherman was surprised to see that General Burnside had taken up headquarters in a fine mansion on Kingston Pike, where the officers were treated to a roast turkey dinner, complete with a regular dining table, a clean tablecloth, dishes, knives, forks and spoons, which was an experience that Sherman had not encountered during the war. After Sherman exclaimed that he had reports of the troops starving, Burnside explained that he had communication with a settlement of Union sympathizers on the south side of the river, who had supplied him with a good amount of East Tennessee staples: beef, bacon and cornmeal.

Thus far, five United States presidents have been guests in this building: Andrew Jackson, James K. Polk, Andrew Johnson, Ulysses S. Grant and Rutherford B. Hayes. The stopover of Rutherford B. Hayes in September 1877 marked the heyday of the social era of the Lamar House. A luncheon was prepared by Mr. and Mrs. James Cowan. Following lunch and a speech given by Hayes, the public was invited to meet and shake hands with the president. He spent two hours greeting the enthusiastic Knoxvillians. That evening, Hayes enjoyed a presidential dinner at the Lamar House, followed by an excursion across the river to a dance at the farm of Perez Dickinson's grand Island Home. Dickinson was a partner in the extremely successful Cowan and McClung wholesaling business. He was from Massachusetts and a cousin of the poet Emily Dickinson.

The Lamar House's position in the community had begun to slowly erode as the railroad developed. Newer, larger and more modern hotels offered comfortable lodging and fine dining, as the commercial activity with the wholesaling warehouses moved city activity north along Gay Street and Jackson Avenue.

In 1908, the ballroom of the Humes building was converted into a theater. The new Bijou Theater opened to a sold-out crowd in 1909, with a production of *Little Johnny Jones* starring George M. Cohan. The Bijou was one of the first theaters in the area to admit both black and white guests. Black patrons had a section in the gallery and entered from a set of stairs near the side of the building. The Bijou enjoyed a run of many successful live theatrical performances.

Construction began in 1926 on the Tennessee Theater, a few blocks down Gay Street. The owners of the Tennessee also bought the Bijou Theater but sold it to an area businessman with the stipulation, or a non-compete clause, that the Bijou would not be used for theatrical productions of any kind for the next five years.

During the era of prohibition, the Bijou Theater became the Bijou Fruit Stand. This "fruit stand" was noted as one of the first establishments in Knoxville to sell bananas. The new, unusual and exotic fruit sold for ten cents each.

In 1934, Knoxville's first Chinese restaurant, the Pagoda, was opened by Max Weinstein in the space. The Pagoda featured an extensive American menu of oysters in season, relishes and appetizers, soups and broths, fish and shell fish (trout, mackerel, shad, snapper, pompano, lobster and shrimp), steaks, veal cutlets, lamb chops, pork chops and tenderloin, fried or broiled ham or bacon, eggs, spaghetti, cold meats including tongue and Chinese roast pork, salads, sandwiches (even a goose liver sandwich), vegetables, seven preparations of potatoes, desserts, cakes, fruits such as "ice cold" watermelon and four preparations of toast. The Chinese menu included multi-course Special Chinese Dinners of soup, entrée,

CHINESE MENU

SPECIAL CHINESE DINNERS

SERVED FROM 12 TO 3 P. M.

No. 1— .75
Noodle Soup
Oriental Chow Mein
Steamed Rice or Choice Veg. Rice Cake
Bread and Butter   Oolong Tea

No. 2—$1.00
Subgum Soup
Chicken Chop Suey
Steamed Rice   Mixed Fruits
Bread and Butter   Finest Tea

No. 3—$1.25
Oriental Soup
Mushroom Subgum Chicken Chow Mein
Foyoung Done
Steamed Rice   Preserved Gamgots
Bread and Butter   Long Soo Tea

SOUPS

Chicken Soup, Clear.................. .20
Plain Noodle Soup................... .20
Chicken with Egg................... .25
Chicken Subgum Soup................ .35

SEA FOOD CHOP SUEY

Fresh Lobster Chop Suey............ .75
Lobster with White Mushrooms...... 1.00
Fresh Shrimp Chop Suey with
White Mushrooms................ .75
Oyster Chop Suey.................... .60
White Mushroom Oyster Chop Suey... .75
Fish Chop Suey..................... .60

CHOP SUEY

Plain Chop Suey.................... .40
Chinese Chop Suey.................. .40
American Chop Suey................ .40
Extra Fine Chicken Chop Suey...... .70
Chinese Chop Suey without Onions.. .50
White Mushroom Chop Suey.......... .60
Vegetable Chop Suey without Meat.. .50
Green Pepper Chop Suey............ .50
Fine Cut Chop Suey................ .50
White Mushroom Fine Chop Suey..... .75
Subgum Chop Suey.................. .75

CHICKEN CHOP SUEY

Chicken Chop Suey.................. .60
Chicken with White Mushrooms...... .90
Fine Cut Chicken Chop Suey........ .75
Fine cut Chicken with white Mushroom .90
Chicken with Green Pepper......... .70
Chicken Subgum................... 1.00
Chicken with Chinese Almonds...... .90

BEEF CHOP SUEY

Beef Chop Suey.................... .50
White Mushroom Beef Chop Suey..... .70

Subgum Beef Chop Suey.............. .90
Beef Chop Suey with Green Peppers.. .60
Beef Chop Suey with Tomatoes...... .60
Pepper Steak...................... .75

VEAL CHOP SUEY

Veal Chop Suey.................... .50
White Mushroom Veal Chop Suey..... .70
Fine cut White Mushroom Veal
Chop Suey..................... .75
Veal Chop Suey with Green Peppers.. .60

CHOW MEIN OF FRIED NOODLES

Plain Chow Mein................... .50
Fine cut Chow Mein................ .65
Chicken Chow Mein................. .75
Chicken Chow Mein for two........ 1.40
Chicken Chow Mein with Mushrooms.. 1.00
Lobster Chow Mein................ 1.00
Lobster Chow Mein for two........ 1.90
Subgum Chicken Chow Mein
Mushrooms...................... 1.25
Subgum Chicken Chow Mein
Mushrooms for two.............. 2.25

NOODLES

Chicken Yat Gor Mein.............. .50
Plain Yat Gor Mein................ .35
Extra Fine Yat Gor Mein........... .50
Warmein........................... .60
Chicken Warmein................... .75
White Mushroom Warmein............ .75
Shrimp Warmein.................... .85
Lobster Warmein................... .90
Young Chow Warmein............... 1.00

EGG FOYOUNG

Egg Foyoung....................... .50
Ham and Egg, Canton Style......... .50
Subgum Egg Foyoung................ .75
Chicken Egg Foyoung............... .75
Shrimp, Egg Foyoung............... .75
Lobster Egg Foyoung............... .90
Pocket Egg........................ .75
White Mushroom Egg Foyoung........ .75

FRIED RICE, CHINESE STYLE

Fried Rice........................ .50
Chicken Fried Rice................ .60
Shrimp Fried Rice................. .60
Ham Fried Rice.................... .75
Lobster Fried Rice................ .75
Subgum Fried Rice................. .65

IMPORTED CHINESE FRUITS

Mixed Preserves................... .25
Gamgot............................ .25
Ginger Root....................... .25
Lichie Nuts....................... .25
Chinese Almond Cake............... .15

IMPORTED CHINESE TEAS

Oolong Tea, per pot............... .15
Long Soo Tea, per pot............. .20
Best Mixed Tea, per pot........... .20

Bread or Rolls and Butter Served With Chinese Orders 10c Extra

AMERICAN MENU

Chinese or American Dinner Party Can be Arranged on Short Notice

OYSTERS IN SEASON

Oysters, per plate................ .40
Oyster Cocktail................... .30
Oyster Stew ½..................... .40
Cream Stew ½...................... .40
Fried Oysters, half... .30 Whole.. .50
Fried Oysters in Butter, Tomato Sauce .75
Broiled Oysters with Celery Sauce.. .75
Broiled Oysters with Mushroom Sauce .80
Oysters au Gratin................. .50

RELISHES AND APPETIZERS

Queen Olives...................... .20
Ripe Olives....................... .15
Celery............................ .20
Cold Slaw......................... .10
Radishes and Spring Onions........ .15

SOUPS AND BROTHS

Vegetable Soup.................... .15
Cream of Tomato................... .15
Chicken Soup...................... .15
Tomato Soup....................... .10
Clam Chowder...................... .20
Purse of Peas..................... .15

FISH AND SHELL FISH IN SEASON

Salt Water Trout.................. .35
Fresh Water Trout................. .35
Tenderloin Trout.................. .35
Broiled Spanish Mackerel.......... .40
Fried or Broiled Shad............. .35
Red Snappe Steak.................. .40
Broiled Pompano................... .50
Shrimp Cocktail................... .30

STEAKS, CUTLETS, CHOPS, ETC.

Small Steak....................... .35
Sirloin Steak..................... .50
Tenderloin Steak.................. .65
Porterhouse Steak................. .60
Special T-Bone Steak.............. .67
Hamburger Steak................... .35
Lamb Chops........................ .35
Pork Chops........................ .30
Pork Chops, breaded............... .35
Pork Tenderloin, Breaded.......... .45
Veal cutlets, Breaded, and Tom. Sauce .35
Veal Chops........................ .35
Veal Cutlets, Plain............... .35
Broiled or Fried Ham.............. .35
Broiled or Fried Bacon............ .35

EGGS—ANY STYLE

Fried Eggs........................ .20
Scrambled Eggs.................... .20
Poached on Toast.................. .25
Omelette with Jelly............... .30
Omelette with Asparagus Tips...... .40
Omelette a la White Mushrooms..... .40
Plain Omelette.................... .25
Ham Omelette...................... .30
Spanish Omelette.................. .40
Cheese Omelette................... .30
Ham and Eggs...................... .30
Bacon and Eggs.................... .30
Spaghetti I, Italienne............ .40

COLD MEAT

Tongue............................ .40
Chicken........................... .50
Roast Beef........................ .35
Chinese Roast Pork................ .35
Boiled Ham........................ .30
Combination Meat.................. .60

SALADS

Fruit............................. .25
Tomato Salad...................... .25

Combination....................... .25
Shrimp............................ .35
Chicken........................... .35
Lobster........................... .50
Potatoe Salad..................... .25
Lettuce with Tomato............... .15
Sliced Tomato..................... .15
Sliced Cucumber................... .15
Head Lettuce, French Dressing..... .25

SANDWICHES

Ham............................... .15
Egg............................... .10
Club.............................. .50
American Cheese................... .15
Ham and Egg....................... .20
Chicken........................... .25
Chicken Salad..................... .20
Roast Pork........................ .15
Western........................... .20
Denver............................ .20
Baby club......................... .25
Goose Liver....................... .15
Tongue............................ .15

VEGETABLES

String Beans...................... .10
French Peas....................... .25
Green Peas........................ .15
Stewed Tomatoes................... .20
Stewed Corn....................... .10
Fried Onions...................... .15
French Fried Onions............... .25
Asparagus Tips on Toast........... .30

POTATOES

Julienne.......................... .15
Lyonnaise......................... .20
Mashed Brown...................... .15
Au Gratin......................... .25
O'Brien........................... .25
Shoestring........................ .15
French Fried...................... .15

DESSERTS, CAKES AND FRUITS

Pie, per cut...................... .10
Sliced Orange..................... .10
Sliced Bananas with Cream......... .10
Iced Watermelon................... .10
Grape Fruit, half................. .10
Strawberries with cream........... .20
Strawberry Shortcake.............. .15
Rice With cream................... .15
Sliced Peaches, with cream........ .15
Cantaloupe, half.................. .10

TOAST

French Toast with Jelly........... .25
Milk Toast........................ .20
Cream Toast....................... .25
Dry or Butter Toast............... .10

COFFEE, TEA, ETC.

Coffee, cup....................... .05
Cocoa, cup........................ .10
Tea, cup.......................... .05
Tea, pot for one.................. .10
Milk, glass....................... .05
Cream, glass...................... .15
Half and Half, glass.............. .10
Ice Tea, glass.................... .05

Any Single Order Served for Two 10c
Extra. Second Cup Coffee free.

Left: Chinese menu, the Pagoda; *right*: American menu. *McClung Historical Collection.*

steamed rice or vegetable, bread and butter and oolong or long soo tea. Seafood chop suey and multiple versions of chicken, beef, veal and even an American chop suey were offered. Other offerings on the Chinese menu were noodles, egg foo young, fried rice and an imported Chinese fruits section, including gamgot, ginger root, lychee nuts and Chinese almond cake.

In 1935, Paramount Pictures took on a thirty-year lease for the Bijou, showing second-run and hold-overs of movies that had previously been shown at the Tennessee. But by 1965, Paramount chose not to renew, and the theater became the Bijou Art Theater, an adult, or X-rated, movie theater.

The rooms of the Lamar House were declared a public health hazard and closed in 1969. The theater, however, continued to operate. In an odd turn of events, in 1971, the Bijou was bequeathed to Church Street United Methodist Church. As newspaper articles began to surface that the church owned a property where burlesque dancing was taking place, the church quickly sought to sell the building.

By 1975, the Bijou Theater had been closed due to unpaid rent and taxes and was slated for demolition. This time, however, the citizens of Knoxville would not be denied. The same year, the Bijou was added to the list of the National Register of Historic Places. A group of concerned citizens assembled, calling themselves Knoxville Heritage—now known as the leading preservation group, Knox Heritage—and launched a campaign to save the Bijou. The theater reopened in 1977.

After years of the community's dedicated attention, continued fundraising efforts and strategic planning and restructuring, the Bijou Theater rose to its height of popularity with regular performances by the Knoxville Chamber Orchestra, Americana and bluegrass musicians, classic and folk rock groups, comedians and one-man shows. The theater was built before amplification, and music writers and journalists passing through town have often commented on the wonderful acoustics at the Bijou. The booking for the wide variety of acts for the Bijou as well as the Tennessee Theater was taken over by A.C. Entertainment, which also produced Louisville's Forecastle Festival and the massive Bonnaroo Music and Art Festival in middle Tennessee. The Bistro at the Bijou, one of the first downtown projects of preservationist Kristopher Kendrick, opened in 1980 and is now owned and operated by esteemed restaurateur Martha Boggs. Two hundred years later, Margaret Humes's assertion that a well-managed business in this space would be successful has been fulfilled many times over. And as I overheard Martha say the other day, "Now it's our turn to take care of it for a while."

CHAPTER 3

1 MARKET SQUARE

PETER KERN'S ICE CREAM SALOON

Peter Kern arrived in Knoxville in 1863, in the midst of the Civil War. A German immigrant, he first landed in New York in the 1850s with plans to practice his trade as a cobbler. Seeking warmer weather, Kern began working his way south. As the war got underway, he enlisted in the Confederate army in the Twelfth Georgia Infantry, in a regiment commanded by Stonewall Jackson. Kern was injured in battle and sent home to recuperate. On his way back to the battle, he was detained in Union-occupied Knoxville. Kern would be released, but under the condition that he remain in Knoxville and not return to the fighting. The industrious Kern decided while he was in town to go into business with fellow German William Heidel. The pair began with a bakery on the corner of State and Main Streets where they made cookies of molasses and flour for soldiers during the war. Kern eventually bought out Heidel's share and moved to a two-story building on Market Square. By 1875, he had become so successful that he was able to build a new three-story building at 1 Market Square.

Kern had his building designed by one of Knoxville's first architects, Joseph Baumann, in the Italianate style. The new store featured a double front, just as it does now. Each floor was 50 by 120 feet and also included a basement. The first floor featured one portion dedicated exclusively to Kern's wholesale business, as he supplied for what was also known as the jobbing trade (distributing goods) over the states of Tennessee, Kentucky, Virginia, the Carolinas and Georgia. Machinery and engines used to manufacture his goods were located in the rear and basement of the

Peter Kern Building. *McClung Historical Collection.*

building. In 1865, Kern was making two hundred loaves of bread a day. By 1901, he was up to seven thousand loaves a day, with a capacity for up to twenty thousand. He employed forty people continuously and sometimes up to seventy-five. In addition to bread, Kern was also producing cakes, candies, ice cream and sherbet.

The other side of the building was the retail department, where Kern sold his French candies, caramels, creams and wedding cakes to the public. He also handled an extensive line of foreign fruits, seafood and, additionally, fireworks. This side of the first floor also featured a soda fountain. Upstairs was the ice cream parlor, or "saloon."

The ice cream saloon featured square, white, marble-top tables for four, outfitted with small bells on each to call for service. The floor was of polished woods of various colors, and the hall featured deep wainscoting of highly polished and variegated Tennessee marble. Paintings and fine engravings were hung on the upper part of the walls, but probably the most striking feature of the room were the crystal chandeliers, which glimmered and reflected light in all colors. Male waiters dressed in black pants, black ties, white shirts and white coats attended to guests. Ice cream and sherbet was available in nearly a dozen flavors, and crowds would often fill the saloon after plays and musical concerts ended at Staub's Theater on nearby Gay Street.

The *Knoxville Journal* cited the redecoration of Kern's in the spring of 1902. It reported that the name Kern was associated with the best of everything. The firm of A. Greenwood & Co. was contracted to do the remodel. The wallpaper used in the main salesroom was the most expensive ever placed on a wall of a business in the city. It was of a pressed leather finish in rich crimson, while the ceiling and other woodwork was painted in ivory white, cream and gold.

Peter Kern passed away in 1907, at the age of seventy-one. His family eventually sold his business to the Brown family in 1920. By 1931, the business had moved to a new factory across the river on Chapman Highway and focused mainly on bread production.

The upper levels of the Kern Building on Market Square were transformed into a hotel in 1981 and opened under the name Blakely House, just in time to host visitors for the 1982 World's Fair. Blakely House was in the European style, with no two rooms exactly alike. That version of the Blakely House didn't last long, but a reprise of at least the hotel name was put forth in 1990 by brothers Joseph and Pat Parisi. The Parisi brothers had previously managed the catering division of a posh Manhattan restaurant called the Water Club. Some of their celebrity clients included musician Phil Collins, journalist Barbara Walters, Brooke Shields's eighteenth-birthday party guests and businessman Donald Trump.

Extensive renovation was necessary before the new Blakely House could open, as there was much damage to the unused building. The rooms of the new hotel featured amenities such as wet bars, refrigerators and ice makers. The Parisi venture also featured a café on the ground floor offering American and Italian specialties. But, alas, the Blakely House was not destined to survive in Market Square. The property was then bought by local developer and preservationist Kristopher Kendrick, who renamed the hotel the St. Oliver, fashioned it with antiques he collected locally and from around the world and took up residence there.

A new concept, the Soup Kitchen, opened on the south side space of the ground floor in 1983. Bob and Jean Bardorf began the business out of a cooking hobby by opening their first restaurant in Oak Ridge in 1980. They offered made-from-scratch menu items as an alternative to fast-food

The
Blakely

Guest satisfaction is our business.

The Blakely is a full service executive hotel located in the heart of downtown Knoxville. The suites are luxurious and the rooms are beautifully appointed. Special requests are our specialty, because your comfort is our pleasure.

The Blakely Cafe presents the return of quiet elegance to dining, with the finest in new American and classic Italian cuisine.

By Choice not Chance.

Corner of Union & Market
Knoxville, TN 37902
(615) 523-6500

Blakely House Hotel and Café ad.
McClung Historical Collection.

eateries. Boasting over 120 soup recipes, including U.S. Senate bean, Hungarian goulash, cheddar shrimp, black bean and rice and fish mornay, they featured seven daily soups; chili; salads; scratch-made fresh-baked breads served hot, such as French, rye, cheese and raisin; and dessert. Guests proceeded through a cafeteria-style line to order.

In 1993, the Soup Kitchen was sold to longtime employee and manager Elaine Graham. In the late 1990s and early 2000s, as the downtown business slowed, Graham decided to take matters into her own hands and bought a couple of trucks to deliver hot lunches to businesses around town. The food truck pioneer sold the business in 2004 after twenty-two years of working at the restaurant.

The Soup Kitchen's new owner, Hossein Ghodrat, changed the name to Market Square Kitchen. While he kept the same basic design, including the cafeteria-style line, new additions included Reubens, barbecue and even an old country store favorite, fried baloney sandwiches. He also added hot breakfast options such as omelets, eggs Benedict and hash browns.

Eddie Cui, a native of China, moved his restaurant Shonos from West Knoxville to the other ground-floor space of the Kern Building in 2003 with the plan of having a lunch spot so that he could attend night classes in order to finish his business degree at UT. It was bad timing for Cui, as the redevelopment of Market Square had just begun, creating a lull in lunch traffic. In 2004, he sold to Willy Rosenberg, who, with his father and son, ran Shonos in City, continuing Japanese hibachi and later adding sushi to remain competitive with the forward-moving food scene of the city.

In 2005, aspiring author Elizabeth Gilbert took a temporary job teaching writing at the University of Tennessee and rented a room for her stay in Knoxville at the St. Oliver. While there, she also finished writing a book. *Eat, Pray, Love* stayed on the *New York Times* bestseller list for 187 weeks and went on to be made into a major motion picture starring Julia Roberts.

Gilbert had a room on the third floor of the St. Oliver that faced the street. She often ate in, using a microwave, small fridge and tea kettle, and created meals of pickles, eggs, carrot sticks, nuts and tea. When her husband joined her, Gilbert mentioned that he found Knoxville to be a marvel of order and civic responsibility. He found a restaurant across the street that featured a $3.99, Back-by-Popular-Demand, All-You-Can-Eat lunch special. After they moved on, Gilbert noted that anytime Knoxville was mentioned, her husband would chime out, "Back by popular demand, all you can eat!"

The restaurant across from the St. Oliver was most likely Macleod's, a Scottish pub in the Arnstein Building that offered daily lunch specials Monday through Friday from 11:00 a.m. to 3:00 p.m., including microbrewed beer from a brewery in nearby Sevierville. Ahead of its time featuring locally brewed beer, Macleod's also holds the distinction of being one of the first five businesses in Knoxville to offer free Wi-Fi. In 2003, Wi-Fi was spreading into medium-sized markets such as Knoxville. Three of the Knoxville Wi-Fi locations were in the downtown area at Macleod's, Preservation Pub and Downtown Grill & Brewery, known to locals at the time as the "BARmuda triangle." The service we now take for granted was installed by the company AirCom, whose owner said he saw Wi-Fi as a test. He wasn't sure if one hundred people would use it and wasn't even sure anyone would use it.

Kristopher Kendrick passed in 2009, and the property was purchased a year later by Ethan Orley and Philip Welker for $1.53 million, with plans to invest another $1.5 million for renovations to the boutique hotel. The renamed Oliver Hotel opened in 2011.

Orley and Welker opened the Peter Kern Library, a speakeasy-type craft cocktail bar, in the hotel lobby. But they were also looking for a new restaurant concept to occupy one of the ground-level spaces that would well serve the hotel clientele and be open and busy all the time. They swayed Asheville-based Tupelo Honey Café to open its first of many locations outside Asheville in the space in 2012. When Shonos unexpectedly closed in 2014, Orley and Welker set to work on opening their own restaurant. The stylish Oliver Royale, with its new American menu, opened in 2015.

PART II

Saloons, Outlaws, Vice
and Vegetables

CHAPTER 4

CAL JOHNSON

FROM SLAVE TO SAVVY SALOON OWNER

*C*aldonia "Cal" Fackler Johnson was born a slave but died one of the wealthiest men in the state of Tennessee, with an estate worth hundreds of thousands of dollars. Cal was born in Knoxville in 1844. He was the son of Cupid and Harriet Johnson, slaves of Colonel Pless McClung. They lived at the McClung residence at 526 South Gay Street, later the site of the Farragut Hotel. Cal's father was very skilled with horses and was known as a respected trainer. When he was fourteen, Cal went to live at the McClung estate at Campbell's Station, about seventeen miles west, now the town of Farragut, where one of his jobs was to help tend to the horses. This work instilled in Cal a lifelong love of the horse trade and, little did he know at the time, helped shape his future endeavors.

At the end of the Civil War, the industrious Cal created a job for himself by submitting the lowest bid for a government contract exhuming bodies from battlefield graves and relocating them to proper cemeteries. Around the same time, he developed a drinking habit, winding up a destitute drunk living on the streets of Knoxville. Cal recognized his plight and was able to turn his life around by getting sober and taking a job as a cook. He later worked as a bartender and, after saving up $180, was able to lease a building on Gay Street from John Horne, a whiskey dealer, to open a small grocery store in 1879.

With the profits from his store, Cal was able to expand and open his first of several saloons. His saloons generally operated under some variation of the name Poplar Log—Poplar Log Branch, Poplar Log Center Branch and later the Lone Tree. His businesses were centrally located at such areas as Gay and Wall Streets, Vine and Central and Gay and Vine. An astute businessman, Cal's saloons served blacks as well as whites, but Cal kept with other customs of the day by not serving women, minors or persons who appeared to be already intoxicated. Cal was noted to not drink in his saloons. Restaurateurs and bar owners soon discover these words from an old moonshiner hold true: whiskey is for selling, not for drinking.

How did a saloonkeeper attract business? Some of them provided hard-to-find newspapers for patrons, but the most common practice noted in many saloons between 1870 and 1920 was to offer the "free lunch" as a way to draw customers. Free lunches did not necessarily occur in the middle of the day; they could also go into evening dinner hours or even breakfast. Think of it as an early form of our modern happy hours. The meal might be anything from very simple to elaborate, with the purchase of at least one and sometimes two drinks. Saloonkeepers relied on the expectations of more than one drink being purchased and of repeat patronage by customers. A simple meal might consist of cold preserved meats, cheeses, beans and stalks of celery or radishes. Something more elaborate might include chili, roast beef, sausages or franks, meatballs, baked fish, oysters or eggs. But always present at the free lunch was something salty to build thirst. Salty snacks might include pretzels, crackers, seasoned nuts, olives, dill pickles or even smoked herring or sardines and rye bread.

Making a comfortable living in the food and drink business, Cal was able to turn back to his true love: horses. Not just any horses—Cal developed a collection of prized Thoroughbreds and racehorses. He purchased the famed mare Lenette in Frankfort, Kentucky, for $6,000. Cal also owned the standardbred trotter George Condit, who was a champion at the Columbian Exposition in Chicago, breaking a world speed record in 1893. Cal developed a horse racing track in East Knoxville and also one in South Knoxville that provided great entertainment to the city and also allowed gambling. Cal's saloons and racetracks were forced to close when strict prohibition laws were established in 1907. Tennessee was the first state to establish any type of prohibition laws, before the rest of the country followed in 1920. Drinking and possession of alcohol were illegal, and because of the gambling associated with it, the general assembly also outlawed horse racing.

The closure of his businesses did not deter Cal from pursuing new projects or in his contributions to the city. Cal also had vast dealings in real estate and eventually opened a movie theater, the Lincoln Theater, on South Central; it was Knoxville's first movie theater for blacks. When

Waiting for returns on prohibition vote, 1907. *McClung Historical Collection.*

Knoxville hosted the Appalachian Exposition in 1910, at Chilhowee Park, just across the street from his former racetrack, Cal made the space available for the first airplane flights in Knoxville. He served on the Knoxville Board of Aldermen for two terms and in 1906 donated a house at the corner of Vine and Patton Streets for the first YMCA for blacks.

A residential neighborhood grew up around Cal's old racetrack in East Knoxville, and the actual track is now known as the street Speedway Circle. Additionally, one of Cal's old buildings is also still standing. In 1898, he built a factory-type building at 315 State Street, which served as the Knoxville Overall Company; it bears his name in a stone near the top of its three stories. The otherwise obscure building made headlines in 2016 when the city imposed a very rarely used historic preservation overlay on the property that sends future building permits for those certain properties of special notoriety to the Historic Zoning Commission, which encourages preservation.

Here's hoping the best for the old building on State Street, a great visual representation of an amazing life. Cal Johnson, born into slavery, made his own way, enjoyed life to the fullest and never looked back.

CHAPTER 5

PATRICK SULLIVAN'S SALOON AND EATING HOUSE

As the railroad was being developed in Knoxville in the 1850s, a large community of Irish moved into town to labor on its construction. The Sullivan family settled in Knoxville, and their son Patrick became one of the most famous Irishmen in town. Since the late 1800s, everyone here has known the name Patrick Sullivan.

Patrick Sullivan was born in County Kerry, Ireland, in 1841. The Sullivan family immigrated to America when he was a child and eventually settled in Knoxville. They were one of the founding families of Knoxville's first Catholic church, Immaculate Conception, where Patrick as a teen helped build the first church building on Vine Avenue. During the Civil War, Patrick enlisted in the Union army and worked as a supply train commander, rising to the rank of captain. When the war was over, he returned to Knoxville and opened his first saloon. Patrick operated out of a small wood-frame building before building his grand and ornate masterpiece at the corner of Jackson and Central in 1888.

Located at the bottom of a steep hill, the turreted building commands the neighborhood. Near the turret are heavily pedimented gables and a seven-bay curved extension that echoes the curve of the sidewalk. In its graceful design, the building seems to fan outward, welcoming guests from every direction.

After the Civil War, the railroad assisted Knoxville in becoming a wholesaling center. Large wholesale warehouses sprang up along Jackson Avenue where the freight from the train cars could be unloaded straight

Patrick Sullivan's Saloon, Annie's *(small gray building to left)* and White Lily Flour Mill *(far left)*. *Library of Congress.*

into the buildings. Wholesale companies featured elaborate showrooms in the front of their buildings to display goods and employed so-called street drummers, who would greet visiting buyers near the trains and guide them to the showrooms. Before or after these business dealings, the street drummers would customarily treat customers to beverages or refreshments. Patrick Sullivan's Saloon was located at the center of trade among Knoxville's wholesaling warehouses and was convenient for such activity. Sullivan's Saloon was known as progressive, selling to both male and female patrons.

A favorite story of some Knoxvillians relating to Patrick Sullivan's Saloon is of the infamous outlaw Harvey Logan, aka Kid Curry, who has been called the wildest of the Wild Bunch Gang, headed up by Butch Cassidy and the Sundance Kid. The head of the Pinkerton Detective Agency, William Pinkerton, called Logan the most vicious outlaw in America, stating, "He has not one single redeeming feature. He is the only criminal I know of who does not have one single good point." After a string of bank and train robberies out west, Logan headed east, somehow ending up in Knoxville.

Having a penchant for alcohol, Logan naturally wound up at Sullivan's Saloon, among others, where he had been drinking before getting into a dispute with another man. When two deputies tried to break up the fight, Logan shot them. He was arrested and held in jail, where as many as five thousand curious Knoxvillians went by to get a glimpse of the notorious criminal. Many of the female visitors even took him food and gifts. Logan mysteriously escaped from the Knoxville jail and was seen riding out of town on the sheriff's horse.

Prohibition forced Sullivan's and all Knoxville saloons to close in 1907. The building was later bought by Mike Armetta in 1921 to house his general store and Liberty Ice Cream Company. Armetta was from Sicily and came to Knoxville to work for the railroad. He first had a store on Market Square but, after returning to Sicily to marry, brought his new bride back to Knoxville and settled on Central. Having no source of refrigeration, Armetta kept his ice cream cold by packing ice around it. Ice was brought into Knoxville by trains and stored in a building across the street from Armetta's. When Armetta closed his shop, he rented the building to an upholstery shop until the 1960s. The neighborhood languished under its reputation as a rough and unsavory part of town. Then, as if by magic, enter again Kristopher Kendrick, who purchased and restored the property.

The costs for the renovations of the four-thousand-square-foot building were nearly $300,000. Kendrick's rehab of the Sullivan Building included incorporating vintage lumber salvaged from other old buildings in the Old City and restored chandeliers. A fifty-foot cherry bar, hewn from a single tree, was installed. The bar stools were covered with remnants of an Oriental rug and fringe. A brass rail separated the bar from the dining tables, whose chairs were from the Andrew Johnson Hotel, and one side of the building was lined with booths from the old Atlanta Café. Stone wedges anchoring the bar came from the old Williams House in Fountain City, which was said to have been modeled after the original saloon. Stained-glass windows were hung above the front doors. The original floor was kept and polished.

The new Patrick Sullivan Saloon opened on St. Patrick's Day 1988, one hundred years after the original saloon had opened. Kendrick insisted on the name of the establishment, noting, "That's what it has to be called, because he built it, and he deserves it."

My tour passes through this area often, and many times I have heard locals reminisce, "Oh, I used to really enjoy eating at Patrick Sullivan's." The fond memories of great meals can be traced back to Frank Gardner, Kendrick's partner in the Sullivan project. Gardner was known for his restaurants

Timberwinds and the Burning Bush in Gatlinburg. His signature dish for Patrick Sullivan's was Shrimp Jameson—Gulf shrimp in a creamy sauce flavored with Jameson whiskey over linguini. The menu also featured Buffalo Bill's Pepper Steak, Filet Oscar, Sullivan's Prime Rib, Crabmeat Shrimp Imperial, Roast Rack of Pork and Porterhouse Steaks. Gardner arranged for seafood to be shipped in fresh from the Fulton Fish Market in New York. An Irish soda bread with caraway seeds was served, as well as fresh-baked croissants, baguettes for chili dogs and rolls for burgers. Daily blue plate specials such as fried chicken and meatloaf filled the lunch hours, and rich, gooey desserts of chocolate bourbon pecan or peach pies, strawberry shortcake, cheesecake and pound cake smothered with strawberries and whipped cream or chess squares—chess pie filling on a cookie crust served warm with ice cream—topped off a meal. Gardner's strategy was to serve ample portions to encourage repeat visits by customers. This tactic worked well in Knoxville.

Kendrick and Gardner used a unique marketing tool for the Old City and their new restaurant by creating a "founders' society" called Sullivan's Clan. The clan was promoted to be for individuals who were interested in the revival of the Old City and restoration of other buildings like Patrick Sullivan's. It featured three types of memberships at different dollar amounts, with the stipulation that the cost of membership was fully redeemable at Patrick Sullivan's in food and drink credits. A Sullivan's Clan plaque was to be displayed with names of all the members. Patrick Sullivan's closed for a short time, but Gardner reopened it in 1999, only to close again in 2011, citing health concerns.

The Lonesome Dove Western Bistro, featuring urban western cuisine by Chef Tim Love, opened in the Patrick Sullivan Building in 2016. Love attended school at the University of Tennessee and got his start working in restaurants in Knoxville. He gained notoriety in 2006 when he defeated Iron Chef Masaharu Morimoto in Battle Chile Pepper on Food Network's *Iron Chef America*. Love has also appeared on Bravo's *Top Chef Masters* and makes regular appearances hosting cooking segments on NBC's *Today Show* and ABC's *Good Morning America*. He starred on CNBC's *Restaurant Startup*, where he had the opportunity to choose new restaurant concepts to invest in. Love has been featured in the *New York Times* as well as *Food & Wine* and *Bon Appétit* magazines, among many others.

From outlaws to celebrity chefs, over 125 years later, Patrick Sullivan's Saloon is still going strong.

CHAPTER 6

THE BOWERY, BIG BISCUITS AND A VEGETARIAN CAFETERIA

I can't imagine the surprised look on my face when a tour guest asked me directions to the Bowery. "The Bowery" is an old nickname that was used for Knoxville's Central Avenue (now our Old City) in its rough and rowdy days of the early 1900s, so far removed from us now that I had rarely even heard someone speak the term. I knew immediately my guest must be from New York City, as this area was nicknamed after a similar raucous neighborhood there. Central Avenue's proximity to the railroad gave it a bit of a transient flavor. Violence and mayhem were once not uncommon here, as the area endured such vices as drunkenness, prostitution, drugs, theft and even murder. It was said you could just as easily find a million-dollar wholesale house as you could a brothel, gambling den or cocaine parlor in this crime-ridden neighborhood.

But, as typical Knoxvillians, some searched out Central Avenue for the big biscuits. An establishment on Central with no name on the building was known as the "Big Biscuit" restaurant. It was so called because the biscuits served there were twice as big as biscuits served elsewhere in town. The biscuits were accompanied by big, thick slices of cured country ham, red-eye gravy, eggs and a steaming, rich, flavored coffee. Syrup was also available on the tables for patrons who wanted to add a bit of sweetness to their breakfast. The price for the meal was fifteen cents and included free refills of coffee. At the time, food prices could be kept low by a glut in the market. Fresh eggs were abundant and could be obtained for as low as ten or fifteen cents a dozen. A buyer could travel out to rural areas where

The Vegetarian Cafeteria. *McClung Historical Collection.*

money was scarce and purchase ham for as low as ten or fifteen cents per pound if he offered cash.

The Big Biscuit served its bountiful meals to both black and white patrons. A thin partition separated the tables. It was common to see policemen near the Big Biscuit in order to keep the peace, as drunken men who had spent a night on the town in the Bowery would often engage in fights during the breakfast service. For a long time, saloons in the Bowery closed at 10:00 p.m., and then later on at midnight, but dance halls, nightclubs and the bordellos of the red-light district on the street adjacent to Central stayed open much later. Horse-drawn taxicabs were available at all hours of the night and provided curtained windows for passengers who preferred not to be seen or recognized in the Bowery.

On the other side of town from the Bowery, some folks were trying to promote a more wholesome, healthy lifestyle by establishing Knoxville's first cafeteria—of all things, a vegetarian cafeteria—in 1922. Dr. E.A. Sutherland, who had been president of Walla Walla University in Washington State and later president of Madison Health Care Center near Nashville, established the Layman Foundation in Knoxville. The others who made up the foundation's board were on the forefront on healthcare and the natural food movement of the day. They operated out of a new building at 507 West Clinch Avenue.

The lower level of the building housed Lovell's Electro Turkish Baths. R.A. Lovell and his wife trained at the Battle Creek Health Center in Michigan. Their hot air baths were similar to a sauna and were followed by a warm-water wash and massage, providing the benefit of cleansing and purifying the body. The upper level housed the Vegetarian Cafeteria. The Layman Foundation had a large endowment of $1 million from Lida Funk Scott, of the Funk and Wagnall family of publishers. They established vegetarian cafeterias in Asheville, Atlanta, Birmingham, Chattanooga, Louisville, Memphis and Nashville similar to the one in Knoxville.

The Vegetarian Cafeteria menu stated that they would be glad to work with customers' doctors who had prescribed a vegetarian-based diet for them. The dining room had seating for one hundred, a serving deck for fast service and a pleasant display area for food. Nuts, fruits, vegetables, legumes, whole wheat grains, milk and eggs dominated the menu. Soups and many varieties of salads were available, as well as mixed fruit salad with whipped cream or a chopped fruit mold. Soy beans, nut-meat and vegetarian potpie could be accompanied by a vegetable loaf, something called vegex gravy and more cream in creamed vegetable dishes. Surprisingly, the health-conscious cafeteria also offered breaded okra. It was the South, after all. Many desserts were also available, including pies made with whole wheat crust, apple dumplings, baked apples, a whole wheat sponge cake with (more) whipped cream, fruit shortcake, Bavarian cream, fig sauce and the pièce de résistance: Prune Whip. Beverages included a fresh spinach juice.

I often say that some restaurants close simply because they are ahead of their time. The Vegetarian Cafeteria, interesting concept that it was, closed in 1928, but it's fun to know that Knoxville once had its own little version of a spa and health food restaurant.

PART III

Boomtown: The Effects of the Railroad

CHAPTER 7

KNOXVILLE EXPLODES

THE NEED FOR LODGING AND DINING

After the arrival of the railroad, Knoxville's biggest need was for hotels with modern amenities and high-quality food. Merchants, buyers, salesmen, travelers, tourists—the trains brought people in from everywhere, and new commerce caused the city to grow by leaps and bounds.

The New Schubert Hotel was built by Herman Schubert in 1875 at the corner of Gay Street and Cumberland. It was noted that the service and especially the cuisine of the New Schubert would be comparable with any first-class hotel in the country. The hotel featured one hundred sleeping rooms, electric lights, well-lit sample rooms (hotels of the day often featured specific rooms as "sample rooms" for traveling salesmen and buyers), bathrooms, billiard and barrooms, a telegraph and transfer office and even a barbershop.

Schubert was well known for his hospitality, making sure his guests felt at home at the hotel, especially during holidays. His restaurant was known as very high quality and featured a beautiful and clever Christmas dinner, with the following menu: Mock Turtle aus quenelle, Consome d Volaille a la Royal, Tennessee Salmon with Lobster Sauce, Southdown Mutton with Caper Sauce, Capon and Pork with Cream Sauce, Stuffed Young Turkey, Hunch of Venison with Current Jelly Sauce, Young Pig with Chestnut Stuffing, Sirloin of Beef a la Joinville, Filet de Beef pique aux Champignons and Petit Pattees of Oysters a la mamande. The game section included Mallard Duck with Chasseur Sauce, and wouldn't every visitor like to try the local Tennessee delicacy of Opossum with a Milk purie of sweet Potatoes? Fried Saratoga Chips note a throwback to a chef's frustration resulting in an ever-loved snack (potato chips were often described by their namesake origin of Saratoga Springs, New York, even into the twentieth century). Macaroni au gratin anse parmesan, Queen fritters a la sabayon, vegetables, salads and Christmas pies and cakes rounded out this wonderful meal.

The Palace Hotel was built by Knoxville mayor Mel Thompson in 1889 at the corner of State and Commerce Streets. It also featured modern amenities and was known for excellent service and cuisine. The Palace was "famous for its table" with the salesmen, travelers and tourists who came through town. Folks were heading north or south and found Knoxville a pleasant stop in between because of the mild seasons and many attractions. The dining room of the Palace had a seating capacity of 125, while the hotel had a sleeping capacity of 180.

The Hotel Vendome, at the corner of Clinch and Walnut, opened in 1890. It was built in the Richardsonian Romanesque style and named for the famous square in Paris. Along with the Palace, the Vendome featured some of the first elevators in Knoxville. The Vendome was described as very elegant and perhaps the most handsome structure in the city at the time. It was turreted, adorned with a stone cascade of balconies and embellished with sandstone carvings. The impressive building was five stories tall, with the dining room specifically located on the fifth floor to be away from the smells of the kitchen. The Vendome's chef was Henri Donnett, from Boston, who had a team of five cooks—three French, one Scottish and one German. Dishes at the Vendome were exclusively French. Lynnhaven en Coquilles, or seafood baked in a scallop shell or a dish shaped in the form of a scallop shell, was a specialty. The dining room was built in an unusual semicircle shape, and each of the arrangements of the tables formed a letter V.

The Hattie House opened in 1881 at Gay and Clinch. A very large hotel, the Hattie House could lodge 250 guests and seat 120 in the dining room. It had the distinction of being the headquarters of the drummers of the wholesale trade, which meant a "superior table" and entertainment would be found there for their clients. Meals from the first-class restaurant could be had at all hours of the day or night. The Hattie House was renovated into the Imperial in 1894. The Imperial's rooms each offered long-distance telephone connections. The Imperial burned due to a lightning strike in 1916 and was replaced with the Hotel Farragut.

C.B. Atkin built two hotels. Atkin got his start in his father's furniture business but then focused on mantels, which were in high demand in the 1890s, as fireplaces were often the main or only source of heat in homes. C.B. Atkin eventually grew his mantel company to 450 employees and was proclaimed "King of the Mantel Makers" in a trade magazine. In 1907, Atkin built the Colonial Hotel on Gay Street, with a furniture factory located in the rear of the building. The Colonial was located next to Staub's Theater and offered seventy-five rooms, forty-five of those with tiled baths. It was one of the first hotels in Knoxville to have automatic sprinklers for fire protection. The café at the Colonial seated one hundred.

In addition to his successful furniture company, Atkin was also involved in real estate and housing developments in Fountain City, just north of Knoxville, and Oakwood, called the "Magic Suburb" with all the city conveniences. But of all his real estate holdings, his namesake Atkin Hotel was considered the crown jewel. The hotel was finished in 1910, in time for the Appalachian Exposition. It had a prime location right across from the Southern Railway Station, at the corner of Gay and Depot. It was said that travelers could get from the train to a room in the Atkin in five minutes. The hotel offered 200 rooms, 135 with baths, and boasted President Howard Taft as a one-time guest. The dining room was managed by the well-known Mary Donahue, who also served as the pastry chef. The Atkin soon became the most fashionable place in town to dine and take afternoon tea. C.B. Atkin had an interest in classical music and invited the city's best musicians to provide music in the dining room. Impressed with violinist Bertha Roth Walburn, Atkin extended her engagement in the dining room indefinitely. She went on to found the Knoxville Symphony Orchestra.

The product line of the C.B. Atkin Furniture Company was sold in stores in every state and in most every community with a population of three hundred or more. By 1958, it was producing eight hundred pieces of furniture a day, with a piece coming off the assembly line every thirty seconds. One cute story relating to the Atkin Furniture Company is that of a Fountain City family who went to New York to buy furniture from an exclusive dealer. When they arrived home, their neighbor asked who the pieces were made by. Turning a chair over, they found inscribed underneath: "C.B. Atkin Furniture Co., Knoxville, TN."

C.B. Atkin was also involved with building the first version of the Bijou Theater, the Burwell Building and the Tennessee Theater, as well as being director of the East Tennessee National Bank, the Appalachian Exposition, Eastern State Hospital and the Tennessee School for the Deaf. Atkin assisted twenty-seven students in completing their education at Hiawassee College, which he also listed as a beneficiary in his will. Passenger train service slowed in the 1960s, and the grand Atkin Hotel was demolished in 1966. But most certainly, the legacy of C.B. Atkin lingers with us still.

CHAPTER 8

HOLIDAY ROAD

FOUNTAIN HEAD HOTEL AND WHITTLE SPRINGS RESORTS

As Knoxville began to prosper with business and commerce, many residents began taking weekend holidays to newly established resorts a few miles north of town. Their mode of transportation was a steam locomotive, not on a regular train line but a so-called dummy line, which would simply travel its designated route, make a U-turn and come right back to Knoxville.

The dummy line started at the Central Market, now known as Emory Place. After the railroad was built, Knoxville grew northward. The Central Market was established in 1889 and consisted of thirty-three stalls in a frame structure. Tenants of the market included Jacob Croissant's meat market, Thomas Owens's fish market, Austin Plummer's produce company and Strother Lynn's grocery. The anchor tenant of the market was an interesting business called the Walla Walla Chewing Gum Company, established by W.D. Biddle. Walla Walla eventually grew to produce 1,200 sticks of gum each minute, around two tons every day. Its gum was marketed by eight traveling salesmen in forty-two states.

The dummy line could make several round trips in a day from Knoxville to Fountain City, then called Fountain Head for its huge spring of crystal-clear, restorative and, some said, healing waters. The spring issued forth from one side of the present Fountain City Park at the base of a cliff of solid rock. There were also other large springs in the area.

The first settlement in what is now Fountain City was by John Adair, through his land grant of 640 acres in 1791. Adair was not the typical frontiersman, as he had been a well-educated lawyer and politician in Ireland and, in America, raised cattle and Arabian horses. Arabian stock was brought to a plantation owner in Virginia by a Saudi Arabian prince, and both George Washington and Ulysses S. Grant acquired horses there. Most likely Adair did too. However, he also played an important role in the Revolutionary War in the fate of America's independence.

Adair advanced $10,000 from the sale of frontier land to John Sevier so that he and his fellow Wataugans could take part in the Battle of Kings Mountain, which Thomas Jefferson noted as the battle that turned the tide of the Revolution. The money was paid back, and later, in service of the North Carolina governor, Adair built a supply depot housing pork, beef, corn and flour for soldiers of the Cumberland Guard, whose duties included escorting migrating families through the wilderness and the "extreme frontier" of this new world.

Fountain Head was known as a healing place and by 1825 had become widely known for its religious camp meetings, associated with the Methodist Church. People would come by the thousands on horseback or by wagons to attend the meetings. The Fountain Head campground was sold in 1885 to the Fountain Head Improvement Company for $1,025. The developers built a three-story hotel the following year overlooking the spring and campground. It featured porches on all three levels. A romantic, heart-shaped lake was also created.

Knoxvillians flocked to Fountain Head in the 1890s. The dummy line was a fun excursion that could be made in twenty-five minutes. Round-trip fare was only fifteen cents. Many families and couples loved to picnic at the lake, but some went for the excellent food at the hotel, where delicious, multi-course meals could be had for fifty cents. Mary Donahue got her start cooking at the Fountain Head Hotel before moving on to the Atkin Hotel in downtown Knoxville.

C.B. Atkin was also involved in the Fountain Head project. He and a business partner purchased the Fountain Head Land Company in 1905 to begin residential development. The dummy line ceased operation the same year, and an electric trolley car was put in its place. The name was changed to Fountain City by the U.S. Postal Service, as a post office was being established and it was revealed there was another post office in Tennessee already using the name Fountain Head.

A promotional ad for Fountain City made claim that it would be a town where (much unlike the raucous Knoxville) the saloon and whiskey store would never be seen. It was intended to be a great center of education, with

Fountain Head Hotel. *Library of Congress.*

the hope that morals could be as pure as the gushing spring water. Fountain City was annexed by the City of Knoxville in 1962.

Whittle Springs Hotel, also just a few miles north of Knoxville, was begun in 1889 and became known as a place for exclusive tourists. After discovering that the water in their wells was mineral water, believed to have medicinal properties, J.M. and wife Nancy Whittle began selling it. In addition to their hotel, they eventually added a swimming pool, pavilion and golf course to the property. This resort had sixty-five rooms and a dining room for one hundred. Their fine cuisine in their restaurant was created from a stock of pure milk, eggs, select vegetables and meats. Music was provided on the pavilion every evening during the summers. Transportation by trolley was available for guests who wanted to go into town to attend concerts or the theater. The golf course was sold to the City of Knoxville in 1930, making it the city's first public golf course. The hotel was razed in 1964.

CHAPTER 9

RETURN TO GAY STREET

THE GRAND HOTEL FARRAGUT

Back in downtown Knoxville, lodging and dining only increased in luxury with the opening of the new Hotel Farragut in 1919. It was owned by Meyer Hotel Interests, which also held the Hermitage and Maxwell Hotels in Nashville, the Winecoff in Atlanta and the Windsor in Jacksonville, Florida. The hotel's namesake was Admiral David Glasgow Farragut, who was born at Campbell's Station, about seventeen miles west of downtown.

Farragut's father was of Spanish descent and his mother Scotch-Irish, but after the death of his mother, he was adopted by Captain (later Commodore) David Porter, who wanted to give him the opportunity to train to be a military officer. At age nine, Farragut became a midshipman in the U.S. Navy. During the War of 1812, so many British ships were captured that Farragut, then age twelve, was put in charge of taking one of the captured ships back to port. He later served in the Mediterranean and Caribbean, fending off pirates, as well as the Mexican-American War.

When the Civil War began, some speculated that Farragut, because of his southern birth and heritage, would join the Confederacy. But after his many years in service in the U.S. military, Farragut knew his loyalty could only be to the Union. He was given the command of the USS *Hartford*, and under his leadership, the Union took the city of New Orleans. The Southern ports were very important to the Confederacy, as that was where supplies were being brought in from abroad by blockade runners. Farragut's next move was to the last Confederate stronghold at Mobile Bay.

Farragut's reputation was as being very aggressive in battle. Upon entering the bay, when the ships began slowing, Farragut asked what the trouble was. The call came back of torpedoes or mines in the water. Knowing there was no turning back or the port would be lost, Farragut issued his infamous statement: "Damn the torpedoes! Full speed ahead!" That declaration is now known as a paraphrase, as another version was recorded by Farragut's son in a biography of his father: "Damn the torpedoes! Four Bells! (speed was ordered using the term bells, and four bells generally meant full power, or, as fast as possible) Captain Drayton, go ahead! Jouett, full speed!" Captain Percival Drayton was a commander on the ship and James Edward Jouett was at the con, or steering. Some reports from the battle even noted Farragut calling out, "Four bells, eight bells, sixteen bells, damn it!" A famous image from the battle is of Admiral Farragut strapped to the ship's rigging, where he had climbed up to get a better view of the action. Captain Drayton, worried of a fall incapacitating Farragut, ordered a seaman to secure him with a line.

One ship was lost, but Farragut was able to secure the port in what is now known as one of the greatest military battles of all time. Admiral Farragut remained on active duty for life, an honor given only to seven other U.S. Naval officers. Over ten thousand people, including President Ulysses S. Grant, attended Admiral Farragut's funeral. Statues honoring Admiral Farragut have been erected near the place of his birth, which is now a community named in his honor; in Madison Square Park in New York City; one made from bronze salvaged from the propeller of the USS *Hartford* at Farragut Square in Washington, D.C.; and at Marine Park in Boston, Massachusetts, where a traveler's review of the statue branded Farragut "the biggest badass in Boston."

So what kind of establishment could be created to represent a man the caliber of Admiral Farragut? With an investment of $900,000, the Hotel Farragut was designed in the Renaissance style and was composed of nine stories and two basements. It was faced with tapestry brick and terra-cotta trim. The construction was reinforced concrete, steel, stone and tile and was touted as absolutely fireproof.

On the ground floor, finishes of Tennessee marble and verde antique marble composed the public rooms. The floor was of Tennessee pink marble and the wainscot of eight feet of walnut. Persian rugs lined the floor in neutral brown tones, and the walls and ceiling were of a biscuit tint. Furniture was upholstered in plush, tapestry and mohair, and individual writing desks were placed in cozy nooks. The draperies were

Left: The Farragut Hotel. *Brian Stansberry.*

Below: Admiral Farragut (*right*) and Captain Drayton (*left*) on the deck of the USS *Hartford*. *Library of Congress.*

of brocatelle, and chandeliers and potted plants added to the atmosphere of the rooms.

There were entrances to the hotel from both Gay Street and Clinch Avenue, with a taxi stand at the Clinch entrance. A large oil painting of Admiral Farragut hung over the clerk's desk. The painting was commissioned by the hotel owners from local artist Lloyd Branson, said to be the first Knoxville artist to be able to make his living exclusively through art. This painting is now in the Calvin M. McClung Collection of the Knox County Public Library and occasionally makes appearances for viewing in special exhibits.

The hotel contained a tailor shop, valet service and barbershop with eight chairs and manicure station. Two businesses rented space on the Gay Street front and three on the Clinch Avenue front; one was a permanent sample room operated by a large wholesale house. Eighteen other sample rooms were also located on the top floor—another nod to the amount of business being conducted in Knoxville.

The kitchen, main dining room and coffee room were located on the main floor. The center of the lobby was utilized for afternoon tea. A bakeshop, as is still common now with much of the baking at our downtown restaurants, was located in the basement. Also located in the basement was a billiard room with fourteen tables. The Hotel Farragut Coffee Shoppe fronted Gay Street from the north end of the lobby. The color scheme of the room was maroon and white. It was fitted with a glass-topped lunch counter with twenty-five stools, as well as tables with glass tops with waitress service. The silver was by Rogers and the china from Grindley.

The coffee room was where guests might take breakfast or a light or even elaborate lunch, and the bill of fare included, in addition to lunch specials and a sandwich menu, fruit and preserves, cereals, à la carte appetizers and relishes, seafood, soups, eggs and omelets, grilled meats, cold meats, vegetables, salads, desserts, cheeses, bread, toast and cakes. Coffee could be taken hot for five cents or (and for those who thought this was a new trend) iced for ten cents. Many other beverages were available, including chocolate or cocoa, Postum (a coffee substitute of roasted grain), White Rock, Canada Dry, Budweiser, C and C, Mission Dry, CC Ginger Ale, Fall City, tea hot or iced, Grade A milk, buttermilk, Poland Water by the half gallon, French Perrier and Coca-Cola.

Breakfast items in the coffee room included local specialties such as stewed rhubarb with cream or skinless figs with cream; comb honey or strained honey; or, a Tennessean's favorite, apple butter. However, to provide and cater to all tastes of their guests of travelers and tourists, the extensive menu

included dry toast, French toast, butter toast, milk toast, cinnamon toast, dipped toast, cream toast; corn, buckwheat or wheat cakes; waffles; fried, poached, shirred or scrambled eggs with kippered (salted and smoked) herring, sausage or chipped beef; or omelets filled with the typical breakfast meats, cheeses, herbs, currant jelly or even chicken liver.

A daily lunch of a meat, two sides and a drink could be had for thirty-five cents. A more elaborate lunch special was offered for sixty-five cents and included a chilled tomato juice and guest choices of soup, an entrée, two vegetables, dessert, rolls or corn bread and coffee, tea, milk or buttermilk. The sandwich menu featured a Farragut Special of grilled bacon, lettuce and tomato with Russian dressing on plain, whole wheat, rye or toasted bread. A three-layered City Club could also be

This page: Coffee Shoppe menu, the Hotel Farragut. *McClung Historical Collection.*

had or, along with the standards of ham, chicken, roast beef or imported Swiss cheese, something a little different such as a beef tongue or sardine sandwich. Consommé was offered hot or jellied. The à la carte menu included pickles and olives but also cocktails. These cocktails were the edible sort of fruit, shrimp or crab meat. Fruit juices and even a kraut juice was available. Tennessee country ham steak was a lunch entrée, in addition to steak, hamburger, lamb or pork chops, chicken, fish, spaghetti with a julienne of ham and even eggs with calf brains. Vegetable choices included asparagus tips and buttered beets, among others, and salads were served with either French or mayonnaise dressing.

This was the era of actual farm-to-table dining before the term was a trend, and it is noted on the menu that all milk and cream was supplied to the hotel by Avondale Farm Dairy. Probably the most important note to patrons at the time was that it was also "under government supervision," or inspected.

Lunch or dinner in the main dining room was an even more sophisticated affair. Classically trained chefs working in Knoxville had the luxury of intertwining fine French cuisine with local East Tennessee fare, and the Hotel Farragut did it easily and with style. Service included lunch and dinner until eight o'clock in the evening.

The main dining room was windowed all along the entire south and west walls. The north wall was mirrored to give the illusion of French windows. The color scheme was pale blue and gold. Onondago Syracuse china with a poppy flower design was used in the main dining room, and the silverware was from Reed and Barton and featured a crest marked Meyer Hotel Interests. Silver sugar trays held loaf sugar, and the glass was optic blown. An orchestra played at noon and in the evening meal hours and was under direction of none other than Bertha Roth Walburn.

The dining room featured table water from that exclusive resort a few miles north, Whittle Springs. Fresh Beluga caviar, domestic caviar and lobster cocktail were some of the lavish starters. Additionally, the Hotel Farragut was the first hotel in Knoxville to serve oysters on shell. Bisque of Oysters Royale could be had by the cup or by the tureen, or guests could indulge in strained gumbo or clear green turtle soup. Yearling lamb, young turkey and ribs of beef graced the menu of Friday, February 14, 1919, along with grilled or broiled red or black bass, sun perch or bluegill and croppie (crappie) fried in cornmeal. Giant asparagus and other vegetables were plentiful, but the Scotch-Irish influence of the early settlers was very evident, as potatoes garnered their own section of the menu. As many as twenty different preparations of potatoes were offered. For dessert, guests could ask a waiter to bring around the tray of fine French pastries to select from or simply take their pleasure in a slice of huckleberry pie with ice cream. Parfaits, puddings, custards, cakes, éclairs, fruit pies, ice creams and water ices rounded out the dessert menu, and a cheese course could even be added on to the end of the meal.

The opening-night dinner of the Hotel Farragut on February 1, 1919, consisted of Blue Points cocktail, bleached celery, ripe olives, salted almonds, Consomme Florida, cream of fresh mushrooms, grilled Spanish mackerel Montepelier, potatoes julienne, breast of Philadelphia capon farcis periqueux, new cauliflower polonaise, potatoes fondants, Salade Admiral Farragut, toasted wafers, glace fantaisie, petits fours and coffee. What a fitting tribute to Admiral Farragut.

After being adapted into office space and then sitting empty for years, the Hotel Farragut went under construction in 2017 to be converted back into its original purpose as a hotel.

PART IV

The Greeks: Shaping a Culinary Landscape

CHAPTER 10

THE ETERNAL GOLD SUN
AND PEROULAS QUALITY FOOD

The 1900s ushered in a new era of restaurants for Knoxville, headed up by an influx of Greek immigrants. "Bob" Alexander was the first Greek to operate a food business in Knoxville. He hailed from Evrytania, a mountain region similar to East Tennessee in topography, in the upper mainland of Greece. In Knoxville, Alexander started out by selling sandwiches and fish cakes until he earned enough money to obtain a big lunch wagon, which he sat up on the corner of Vine and Central Avenues. He eventually closed his lucrative food business and moved back to Greece. Word of Alexander's success in Knoxville carried through his homeland as an encouragement for others to seek their fortune here.

James Evras and business partner Angel Karras, both of Evrytonia, opened the Market Lunch in 1900. Basil Apostolis and his brother-in-law Athan Zamyozes arrived in Knoxville in 1904 and opened the Busy Bee restaurant, which prospered so much that they also secured the food concessions in the city park. Additionally, they operated the Roosevelt Sandwich Shop on Gay Street. But it was 1907 when two brothers opened a restaurant that would last over seventy years. The Gold Sun became a haven for young Greek men who wanted to learn the restaurant business in America.

The Paskalis brothers opened the Gold Sun Café at 37 Market Square, in a former wholesale liquor store that had been run by Confederate "General" John F. Horne. Market Square was a very bustling area, especially because of the new addition to the Market House, making it the third-largest open market facility in the nation at the time. Farmers would often arrive on

Friday, stable their horses on Vine and Central Streets and then bed down themselves in doorways along the square in order to be ready for the early Saturday crowds.

Two of the young men who came to learn the restaurant trade at the Gold Sun were Nick Caracostis and his first cousin John D. Cavalaris. In 1926, they bought out the Paskalis brothers. The Gold Sun specialized in home-style cooking, but Caracostis and Cavalaris always prepared a daily special dish, generally including lamb, for their Italian and Syrian friends. If a guest wanted fish, one of the cousins would run out to acquire it at the fish market in the Market House. Early on, they sold hamburgers for five cents, fish sandwiches or chili for ten cents and beef stew for fifteen cents. A steak dinner with three vegetables, a dessert and drink could be had for twenty cents, or fifteen cents without the meat. T-bone dinners were twenty-five cents. Frying hens were scarce and only available for purchase in the spring of the year, so an order of fried chicken would run seventy-five cents.

The Gold Sun was one of many establishments that offered Knoxville's first specialty food dish: the Full House, a tamale smothered in chili, often sprinkled with onions and served with saltine crackers. The story goes that the tamale was brought to Knoxville by Harry Royston, who grew up in Greeneville, Tennessee, but ran away with the circus as a teenager. Royston learned about the portable tamales through his travels and work as the concession manager of the circus. The Full House was a very popular dish served in many restaurants beginning in the early 1900s and continuing through today, though it is not nearly as prevalent or easy to find these days.

Over the years, the Gold Sun hosted celebrities such as Olympic track and field gold medalist and ten-time LPGA golf champion Babe Didrikson and her husband, Greek professional wrestler George Zaharis; bandleader Guy Lombardo; and champion boxer Jack Dempsey. Pulitzer Prize–winning author Cormac McCarthy wrote in his novel *Suttree*, set in Knoxville in 1951, about his character, Harrogate, visiting the Gold Sun Café, where "supper plates were being sopped clean," and again "sitting among the morning smells of fried sausage and eggs." Critically acclaimed author David Madden also wrote in his novel *Bijou* of the Gold Sun Café.

The country music stars came too. Country music played a big role in downtown Knoxville, and vice versa. Knoxville is sometimes called the "Cradle of Country Music" because much of the beginnings of country music happened here. Tennessee's first radio station, WNOX, was located in Knoxville and hosted the live radio show the *Mid-Day Merry-Go-Round*, which broadcast from the Market House on Market Square in 1936. The

Thanksgiving menu, 1959, the Gold Sun Café. *McClung Historical Collection.*

Market House was so large that it housed an auditorium on the second floor where people could go to listen to music during the day. After the show, musicians such as Roy Acuff, Archie Campbell, Chet Atkins and others would congregate at the Gold Sun.

In later years, the only star to continue coming to the Gold Sun was Archie Campbell. There was a story behind Campbell's loyalty. In 1937, Campbell came into town from Bulls Gap (about an hour east) to try to find a job playing guitar and singing. Unable to earn enough money for a meal or lodging, on a cold night Campbell walked the streets of Knoxville until he saw the lights of the Gold Sun. (The Gold Sun, like some other eateries of the time, stayed open twenty-four hours.) He went in to warm up, and the staff let Campbell spend the night and fed him doughnuts and coffee. Upon leaving the Gold Sun the next morning, Campbell ran into a cousin who took him to WNOX, which was the beginning of Archie Campbell's long career as a musician, recording artist, actor, writer and comedian.

John Cavalaris's daughter married a young man she had met while in Greece, James Peroulas. After the death of Cavalaris, James became a partner in the Gold Sun. Upon the retirement of Caracostis, James brought in his brother, Frank, as his new restaurant partner. In 1977, James and Frank decided on a change in the atmosphere, look and even name of their restaurant. After seventy years as the Gold Sun, Peroulas Quality Food opened to an overflow crowd on May 16.

Just near Peroulas Quality Food, the Tennessee Valley Authority was opening its new, modern office towers on Wall Avenue. The space had formerly been the T.E. Burns Co., one of the largest retail grocery stores in the country from the 1900s until 1940. The innovative grocery featured cold storage rooms, refrigerated showcases, a bakery and a lunch counter that prepared hot meals but also box lunches for folks to take back to work with them to downtown stores, offices and warehouses. Some specialties at T.E.

Gold Sun Café menu. *McClung Historical Collection.*

Burns were Lady Baltimore Cake and Imperial Salad Spread of boiled ham or bologna, pimentos, cabbage, onion, cucumbers, red and green peppers, sweet pickles and mayonnaise.

With the opening of the Tennessee Valley Authority's new towers, the Peroulas brothers wanted to update with the times. A lowered ceiling and hanging plants were added. New booths in wood and blue lined the left wall, while woven blue chairs graced the middle dining area. One new idea the Peroulas brothers brought to Knoxville dining was a desire to promote local artists by installing an art exhibit featuring paintings by Tennessee artists. On another wall, nostalgic pictures of Knoxville dating back to the 1900s were hung. Both of these décor ideas are still incorporated in many of our downtown restaurants.

The new menu of Peroulas Quality Food featured traditional American food but also three Greek dishes completely new to the city. The "Yeero" (gyro) required a special tower rotisserie machine, which was placed out in the open for customers to view it spinning and cooking. The tender beef was prepared with onions and parsley and served with tomato and special sauce and topped with sour cream on pita bread. The pastitsio, or pastichio, was a sort of Greek lasagna made with layers of pasta, cheese and a meat sauce topped with egg and cream or a béchamel sauce. The souvlaki plate consisted of spiced and broiled chunks of pork tenderloin on skewers served in a cone of pita bread.

Gus's menu. *McClung Historical Collection.*

The basic principles of the Greeks in their businesses were quality, good value, friendly service and cleanliness. The service at Peroulas was known as very fast and efficient. Even though it was a relatively small restaurant, smart time management assured guests they never had to wait long for a seat even during the busy lunch hour. The restaurant was also described as very clean, "spotless, in fact."

By the 1980s, James had noticed a decrease in the downtown business, noting that rural residents had stopped coming downtown altogether. Peroulas Quality Food served its last customers on December 23, 1995, as James, then seventy-eight, and Frank, sixty-eight, decided to retire. Perry and Susan Starkey moved their restaurant Perry's to the location from their space at 29 Market Square in 1996. By 1999, they closed Perry's, citing loss of business due to TVA layoffs and the closing of Watson's department store. "There's almost no reason left for people to come to Market Square," Perry Starkey related. Charlie Jetter then moved Gus's restaurant from Gay Street into the space. The building was sold in 2008 and partially remodeled in 2009.

James Peroulas made a prediction about downtown Knoxville: "Eventually, the people will come back, I just don't know if I'll live to see it or not." They are back, Mr. Peroulas; I wish you could see how the old Market Square is bustling again now.

CHAPTER 11

A REIGN OF REGAS

Our history is written in the hearts or esteem of our satisfied patrons. As long as they're pleased with us in that respect, the rest I consider of little importance." This quote from Frank Regas seems to say it all. Mention the name Regas in a conversation, and a sort of reverence enters the air. The Regas brothers developed such an excellent reputation in Knoxville that the very name Regas implies outstanding service, exceptional quality, good value and the finest in dining.

There were three Regas brothers who immigrated to Knoxville from Greece: Frank, George and Harry. Their character was greatly admired, and they were known as people of great discipline, putting the love of home next to God and hard work ahead of all occupations. It was said that each of the brothers gained the highest opinion of those who patronized and had dealings with them. Frank, in particular, became a leader in the community.

Frank's father had asked him what it would take for his teenage son to be happy and fulfilled, and Frank replied going to "the States," the land of opportunity. His father sent him over at age fourteen with $100. George arrived later, and the two traveled and visited many cities before settling in Knoxville, working a brief while on the railroad.

On July 7, 1919, Frank and George Regas started their first restaurant, the Astor Café, at the corner of Gay Street and Magnolia Avenue. The café was located near the busy Southern Railway Depot, on the bottom floor of the Watauga Hotel. Their younger brother, Harry, arrived to the States later and opened his own place, Regas Coffee Shop at 1701 West Cumberland, at the corner of Seveneenth Street.

Frank and George's Astor Café featured an eighteen-stool counter, split in the middle; six tables; and six booths. The name was soon changed to Regas Brothers Café. The 1930s brought a remodel that expanded their service area to almost double, just in time for their eleven-year anniversary. The special menu for their anniversary week featured multicourse special meals such as guest's choice of vegetable soup à la julienne or grapefruit cocktail surprise and choice for their entrée of a half chicken southern style, a sizzling filet mignon or lamb chop with Florentine sauce. Accompaniments were fresh string beans au gratin, new potato chips and a Golden West salad with Roquefort cheese dressing. All of this, plus dessert of cherry pie or strawberry sundae and coffee, tea or milk, could be had for fifty cents.

Harry's place also featured those famous sizzling steaks and new favorites such as toasted barbecue sandwiches. Harry's Club Breakfasts were "toned to perfection," with JFG Coffee flavored with Southern Dairies cream. Regas Brothers Café served Club Breakfasts too, which might consist of juice, fruit, cereal, two eggs, bacon, toast and coffee for thirty-five cents; hot cakes or waffles with sausage and coffee for twenty-five cents; or fruit, country ham, eggs, toast and coffee for fifty cents.

By 1938, the name Regas Brothers Café had been altered to simply Regas Restaurant. Frank and George emphasized their moderate prices coupled with their excellent food and service, noting that nothing was too good for the people who ate with them. Frank's son William, or Bill, along with George's son Costa, or Gus, helped out in the restaurant. Frank, who knew how to do every job in the restaurant, encouraged the boys to learn a good work ethic early, stating that all work was honorable. They were expected to do the best they could at any task, with Frank's encouragement that there was no such thing as failure, only "CBE's": Character Building Experiences. This established the culture in their restaurants.

Frank was considered a friend of every man. If someone was down on their luck and needed a meal, he would ask them to work an hour to pay for it. He also installed a two-beer-per-customer policy.

A Regas brochure featured a nutritional guide, facts about Knoxville, driving distance to major cities and a map encouraging travelers to visit Regas after their trip to the Great Smoky Mountains or Norris Dam. The brochure also stated that wholesome food was prepared by the most sanitary methods. Western meats, Tennessee milk-fed chickens and famous Tennessee genuine country hams were touted, along with an invitation for public inspection of the kitchen at all hours.

4 Banquet Rooms in Extension
The 4 Banquet Rooms are called the Flower Room, Old Salem, New Orleans, and Woodmere Rooms, accommodating parties of 10 to 150.

The Main Dining Room with its Distinctive Atmosphere Makes Dining Enjoyable.

Our Coffee Shop is Designed for Quick and Efficient Service.

YOU ARE INVITED TO VISIT OUR NEW KITCHEN AT ALL HOURS AND SEE HOW THE FOOD IS PREPARED

We have one of the finest Kitchens in the South—all Electric Pressure Cookers with modern equipment; all Stainless Steel Tables and Vats; all dishes are washed at temperature of 140 degrees, dishes and glasses rinsed and sterilized at 180 degrees, cooking utensils rinsed at 180 degrees.

This page and opposite: Regas Restaurant brochure. *McClung Historical Collection.*

Harry continued operating his restaurant, assuring his guests of cleanliness and quality at all times, until his death in 1948. Both Frank and George passed in the 1950s. Their sons Bill, Gus and Frank G. continued running Regas, with Bill as chairman of the board. Tablecloths, candlelight and fine dining followed soon after.

Harry's son Charles and his wife, Gisela, opened their own restaurant, Regas on Seventeenth (Charlie's Place), in 1966, at the same location where his father and mother had operated Regas Coffee Shop. Prime rib au jus in a six-, ten- or twelve-ounce cut was the specialty of the house at Regas on Seventeenth. It was also available thinly sliced on a sandwich. Other entrées included a veal cutlet with meat sauce, fried or broiled flounder, beef kabobs, barbecue pork, spaghetti, quiche and even vichyssoise. Another interesting dish was called Chicken and Things, which was an open-faced sandwich of two baked chicken breasts, topped with ham and melted Monterey jack cheese and covered with a honey mustard dressing. Hot apple pie topped with cheddar cheese was one of the rich dessert offerings. Charles sold Regas on Seventeenth in 1985 and joined his cousins working at the downtown Regas.

In 1980, Bill became the president of the National Restaurant Association. In his travels around the country, he learned about all the new trends in restaurant dining. This led to the creation of a new restaurant, Grady's Goodtimes, for which the business plan was the work of Bill's son Grady Regas.

Call it an extreme intuition or just extreme good luck, but in the 1940s, Frank, George and Harry bought thirteen acres of farmland west of downtown, which included property along Kingston Pike. It was a real estate deal that would become increasingly sweet over time, as the majority of the population of Knoxville began to move to the west side of town.

In 1982, Grady's Incorporated was formed with Bill, Frank, Grady and Gus Regas. Mike Connor was recruited from Dallas to return home to Knoxville to help start Grady's Goodtimes. Mike invited his college friends Rick Federico and Kevin Thompson to round out the concept development and original management teams. Brothers Will and Ernest Leija led the culinary team, which prepared each recipe from scratch. Steve Puleo, who had worked with Charlie Regas at Regas on Seventeenth as well as with Frank G. Regas at Regas Restaurant, was later brought on as executive chef. The team eventually even included a young Randy Burleson as a marketing intern. Burleson became an outstanding all-around "Goodtimer" (team member), a developer of new team members and was noted as having an

Charlie's Place ad. *McClung Historical Collection.*

unquenchable hospitality energy. Grady's Goodtimes, a 6,500-square-foot restaurant at the corner of Kingston Pike and Papermill Drive, was the Regas family's foray into the trendy full-service casual dining restaurant segment.

In addition to the traditional Greek ideals of good food, service and value, atmosphere was also emphasized at Grady's Goodtimes. The restaurant was designed to be lighthearted and to appeal to the younger age group of singles, young professionals or young married couples. Whimsical kite streamers hung in one dining area, while softly draped quilted canopies hung in another. The décor included oak woodwork, brass, wrought iron and, of course, those green plants so common in the '80s. Interestingly enough, brick arches that were detailed after some in the old warehouse district downtown were a focal point.

At Grady's, the same menu was used at all times—lunch, dinner and Sundays—and emphasized "the good old days when food preparation and service knew no shortcuts." All soups, salad dressings and desserts were made from scratch, and even the coffee was ground in house. Steaks, baby back ribs and seafood dishes were available, as well as burgers and sandwiches, which could be accompanied by Grady's signature side item, tater twirls. Grilled chicken pasta, cheese toast, broccoli cheddar soup, fried chicken tenders and chocolate bar cake were noted as guest favorites.

The "GOOD TIMES, GOOD FOOD AND DRINK" were rolling as Grady's quickly grew in popularity, but a fateful encounter in 1988 would change the course of the company. Bill Regas and Connor were attending a restaurant convention in Dallas and dropped by the Chili's corporate office to seek advice on how to expand. CEO Norman Brinker was listening in on the meeting and suggested that they could grow Grady's better together. As simply as that, the deal was made, and Brinker's company purchased Grady's. They grew Grady's to fifty-two locations but, by 1995, were ready to sell. The Regas family pursued purchasing Grady's back, but in the end, as simply and as devastatingly as that, Brinker International Inc. sold Grady's to one of its largest franchisees, Quality Dining Inc., of South Bend, Indiana, for $70 million, cash.

But much success came to those who were involved with developing Grady's. Mike Connor went on to found Connor Concepts, with the incredibly successful restaurants the Chop House and Connors Steak & Seafood, in six states throughout the Southeast. Rick Federico eventually became the CEO of P.F. Chang's China Bistro, taking the company public and launching Pei Wei Asian Diner, the company's fast casual concept. Steve Puleo founded his namesake, Puleo's Grille, which grew to five locations and was named best restaurant in East and Middle Tennessee numerous times. Steve was also voted best chef for several years. Randy Burleson opened his signature Aubrey's restaurant, built it to nine locations and has been responsible for saving some of Knoxville's favorite eating establishments—Stefano's, Barley's, Sunspot, Bistro by the Tracks and Crown & Goose—by adding them to his portfolio. Grady became the CEO of Regas. The Regas family opened a new restaurant in 1998, right next door to the Grady's at Kingston Pike and Papermill, called Harry's. The last Knoxville Grady's location closed in the early 2000s.

The theme of Harry's was 1940s supper club, featuring an upscale atmosphere and live music. The chef was Bruce Bogartz. A former executive chef at Warner Brothers resort in Aspen, Colorado, Bogartz was familiar with cooking for entertainers, entertainment executives and their clients and immediately became a favorite chef of the Knoxville dining scene. Bogartz's faithful devotees followed him to Harry's, where he also hosted a "culinary academy" to draw in patrons.

Meanwhile, the City of Knoxville was creating a development downtown along the Tennessee River. It received eleven offers for a restaurant space in what was to be the new Volunteer Landing. The Regas family attended every single meeting with the city concerning the waterfront space. Their devotion to being involved in the project impressed the developer. "In our heart of hearts, we always hoped it would be Regas. Whatever we could do to make it work with Regas is what we wanted to do," their spokesperson commented. Riverside Tavern by Regas opened on Volunteer Landing in 1999.

Bill and Grady went on a recruiting mission to Newport Beach, California, with the intent of luring Culinary Institute of America–trained chef Kelli Lott away from her post as executive chef of Wolfgang Puck's Café and back to her home of Knoxville. The trip was successful, and Lott agreed to return to become the executive chef at Riverside Tavern. Steve Puleo was brought in to collaborate with Lott and her collection of chefs to complete the culinary team at Riverside Tavern. The "California influence" was evident in the wood-burning pizza oven, wood-fired rotisserie and grill and even stir-fry vegetables in cucumber peanut sauce. Hey—California. Salmon, tuna, crab and a fish of the day joined Appalachian favorites such as beans with chow chow, onions and corn bread. A tall, light orange velvet cake was created to appeal to sports fans from nearby University of Tennessee and Neyland Stadium.

My friends and I loved the Taverns—dining on the deck of Riverside Tavern before symphony concerts, Westside Tavern (which Harry's eventually morphed into after a brief stint as Regas Brothers Café), was our go-to birthday celebration place, home of our "birthday tuna." Parkside Tavern, Lakeside Tavern—if there was a Tavern associated with Regas, you could find us there.

Regas downtown continued on through all the other projects with its signature prime rib of beef, roasted all day in a special oven. Other specialties included lamb chops, pork tenderloin, seafood salads and platters, as well as New Zealand lobster tails, Cockenoe Bay oysters, Boston scrod, a colossal shrimp cocktail and crab cakes. Salads were served in chilled pewter bowls with homemade dressings of French, creamy bleu cheese, thousand island or the house blend of oil, vinegar, honey and special herbs. Fresh baked breads were served with every meal—whole wheat rolls with the salads and rich, flaky croissants with the entrées.

The future of the original Regas appeared prosperous as nearby Jackson Avenue was talked of as the possible site for the new convention center. However, when the Public Building Authority announced the World's Fair Park for the site of the new convention center and Interstate 40 work changed access to the front of the restaurant, the fate of Regas was sealed. Regas Restaurant closed in 2000.

Always looking ahead, Grady Regas ventured into the brewpub scene. What, you thought going to a brewery in Knoxville was a new thing? In the late 1800s, the old Knoxville Brewery at the corner of McGhee and Chamberlain produced twelve thousand barrels of beer per year before being shut down by prohibition, but the Smoky Mountain Brewing

Above and opposite: Regas Restaurant brochure. *McClung Historical Collection.*

Company, owned by Patrick and Beverly Lucas, was the first brewpub to open in Knoxville, in 1994, at 424 South Gay Street. The couple bought the old Woodruff building and spent an estimated $2 million on renovation, construction and equipment before filing for bankruptcy the following year. Chris Delph acquired the property for $850,000 and opened the Great Southern Brewing Company in 1996. Delph closed the business in 2000. Grady Regas then opened City Brew in the same location.

In 1997, early in the craft beer craze, and at the strong urging of the Knoxville Chamber of Commerce, Grady invested in the resurrected New Knoxville Brewing Company, just down the street from Regas Restaurant at 708 East Depot Avenue (later Saw Works Brewing). New Knoxville Brewing Company products were offered at Regas Restaurant, Harry's Steak and Seafood by Regas, Riverside Tavern by Regas and then at City Brew.

In addition to brewing beer at City Brew, Grady naturally took everything up a notch with the food. But the time was still not right for the Gay Street location. It may have been just a year or two too early, but it was still too early. City Brew closed in 2001. I'm regretting that I missed out on Nantucket crab dip, bratwurst cooked in blonde ale, stout potatoes au gratin and red apple sauerkraut. But perhaps our hearts could really ache for the Chocolate Godiva Pinwheel—rich chocolate cake with a truffle-like filling, rolled, sliced and topped with whipped cream—or a warm peach and cherry bread pudding. But by 2002, Market Square had an $8 million redevelopment plan,

there was a proposed new cinema for downtown, the Tennessee Theater was scheduled for a $20 million renovation and the Sterchi Building was set to open to more than two hundred residents. The Downtown Grill & Brewery easily slipped into the already renovated Woodruff Building in 2002.

In a surprising twist in the ever-changing restaurant world, by early 2001, the original Regas Restaurant was set to reopen, operated by Bill Regas, Mike Connor and Kevin Thompson and fueled by an investment from an old friend of Bill's, Dave Thomas. The Regas family was moved by the outpouring of love and affection from guests during the closing of Regas and realized how much it meant to the community. Guests through the years told their stories of special times spent at the iconic restaurant. One guest related a story about eating at the Regas counter when Bill Regas was about seven years old. Bill stood on a box to use the cash register, and when the guest complimented him on never making a mistake, he replied, "We've all got to learn what to do and to do it well." The revamp was a throwback to the prosperous '80s with the return of pewter plates and bowls to the dining room, and even the Regas trademark cheese cart, where guests were encouraged to carve their own slices of cheese while waiting, was returned to the lobby. I remember being fascinated by that large wheel of cheese—what an unforgettable display!

Over its ninety-year span, Regas grew to 350 seats in the restaurant and could accommodate another 100 in its Gathering Place Lounge. In his dedication of Regas Square, an entire city block named in honor of the famed restaurant, Knoxville mayor (later Tennessee governor) Bill Haslam

Left and below: Regas Restaurant ad. *McClung Historical Collection.*

A TRAVEL/HOLIDAY AWARD WINNING RESTAURANT

◊ Fresh Seafood
◊ Aged Beef
◊ Freshly Baked Breads
◊ Homemade Desserts

July 7, 1919

Reservations: 637-9805

Regas ®

The Restaurant — The Gathering Place

Exit I-40 at Business Loop (Downtown Loop),
turn right at Summit Hill, then right at Gay Street.

called Regas the quintessential American dream and noted that it was the longest-operating restaurant in the state of Tennessee. Over the years, in addition to families and business and political leaders, Regas hosted many performers and entertainers passing through Knoxville. Some of the most memorable were the charismatic Elvis Presley and the flamboyant showman Liberace, who loved the Regas red velvet cake so much that he would always order two pieces, perhaps an homage to his famous motto, "Too much of a good thing…is wonderful!"

On December 31, 2010, the downtown Regas closed for good. The space was then taken by the Knoxville Leadership Foundation, a center for nonprofits providing training, resources and meeting space. Construction of Regas Square, a six-story, 101-unit luxury condominium complex, began in 2017. The Westside Tavern by Regas closed in 2005, and Riverside Tavern by Regas was sold to Ruth's Chris Steakhouse.

The Regas Restaurant was definitely a family affair but also included one somewhat adopted family member: Dave Thomas, who went on to found the Wendy's fast-food restaurant chain. Thomas got his start working in a grocery store, followed by a stint at Walgreen's drugstore on Gay Street, but finally found his niche in 1941, when he began working at Regas Restauarant. The twelve-year-old fibbed about his age to get the job and rode the bus into downtown Knoxville every day to work. Thomas's adoptive family had moved to the nearby "Secret City" of Oak Ridge during World War II. He worked the counter alongside Bill Regas, who was sixteen at the time. Workers on their way to Oak Ridge would stop at Regas for breakfast and then have Bill and David make up sandwiches for them to take for lunch.

Thomas noted that he learned the basics, and at Regas, "everything was done professionally, and I liked it." The Regas family became mentors to Thomas, teaching him the values of honesty and doing things the right way. Thomas recalled Frank Regas telling him, "You can do anything, if you try," and when his family was getting ready to move, George told him, "You've always got a job here, anytime you want it." Thomas replied that he was going to have a lot of places of his own someday.

After the war was over, Thomas's family moved to Lake City. Thomas joined the army and then finally settled in Fort Wayne, Indiana, and found himself working at a barbecue restaurant when none other than Colonel Harland Sanders dropped in on a promotional tour. Thomas's boss purchased a Kentucky Fried Chicken franchise in Columbus, Ohio, and then six years later sent Thomas there to take over the four failing restaurants. In Dave Thomas style, he turned the restaurants around and sold them back to the founder for $1.5 million in 1968, making him a millionaire at age thirty-five. The next year, Thomas opened his first Wendy's in Columbus, Ohio. Wendy's was named after Thomas's daughter Melinda, who was known to her brother and sisters as "Wenda."

In the 1980s, Wendy's grew to be the third-largest fast-food franchise in the nation, just behind McDonald's and Burger King, with six thousand stores. Who can ever forget Wendy's famous ad campaign with commercials featuring Clara Peller's demand, "Where's the beef?!" Other successful ads for Wendy's actually featured Thomas in the commercials to emphasize that the company was built based on his image and with his ideals of hard work, quality and good value.

Despite his success, Thomas only had an eighth-grade education. It wasn't until 1993 that he earned a high school equivalency certificate. His classmates had some fun with it and voted Thomas "Most Likely to Succeed." Thomas also wrote two books, *Dave's Way and Well Done,* and donated all the proceeds of sales to the Dave Thomas Foundation for Adoption. He noted in his books that if he could give anyone advice, it would be to find a mentor, just as he had in the Regas brothers, and that if the reader only took away one thing from his books, he wanted it to be the importance of honesty. "You can't deal with people that aren't honest. Honesty and integrity can't be replaced."

When *Fortune* magazine approached Thomas about doing an article on him, he invited the editor to Knoxville to see where he had learned the values that made him successful: honesty, integrity and respect for others. On visits to Knoxville, it was noted that Thomas constantly teased Gus Regas and always referred to him as Costa, his given name, noting a familial intimacy. Thomas said that at Wendy's, "our objectives are quality, cleanliness, service, and value, and that's no different than when I worked right here. That was the message in 1944, and that's the message in 1994." Over and again through the years, Thomas referred his success back to the Regas family. "I owe it all to my roots in Knoxville, and my work at the Regas Restaurant."

Frank, George and Harry Regas—their influence spread all throughout their community, the Knoxville dining scene and well beyond. Nicely done, gentlemen, nicely done.

CHAPTER 12

CONSIN AND KOTSIANAS

*G*reek people have a lot of determination," remarked George Consin, who had immigrated as a child with his family to the United States from Greece. Beginning at ten years of age, he worked in his father's Greek restaurant in Woodstock, Virginia. Upon moving to Knoxville in 1937, Consin worked at the old Sanitary Lunch on Gay Street, where he cooked, washed dishes and scrubbed floors for three years before opening his own business, the Gay Grill. He only took one year off to serve with the U.S. Maritime Commission during World War II but was discharged after suffering serious injuries aboard a ship and the doctors told him he would never walk again. Consin proved them wrong and was soon back to work running the Gay Grill.

Although he had graduated from college with a degree in engineering, Consin enjoyed the restaurant business. Feeling that his life's work would be in the food industry, Consin determined there was a need for a Tennessee state association for restaurant operators. After learning that Colonel Harlan Sanders had established one in Kentucky, Consin called on him and Frank Regas, and they formed an association in Knoxville, which was the first in the state. The three movers and shakers then traveled to Chattanooga, Nashville and Memphis and established associations there.

By 1950, the Knoxville Utility Board was expanding its office on Gay Street—right into the space of the Gay Grill. Consin quickly found a bigger and even better space right across the street, where he reopened under the name of the Garden, which he operated there for the next twenty-three years.

That engineering degree did eventually come in handy, as in the 1960s, Consin designed and obtained a patent on a device intended for use in restaurants, which he called the Hyd-A-Rak. The mechanism was a disappearing tray stand that would retract out of sight under a table or booth, aimed at saving servers millions of steps. A salesman friend of Consin helped take the product as far as Hawaii and Alaska and even internationally to Germany and South Korea.

Consin ventured slightly south of downtown, just across the river, in 1971 when he opened the Carriage House restaurant at 4009 Chapman Highway. It was a large Colonial structure that featured three dining rooms and served breakfast, lunch and dinner. The noted specialties at the Carriage House were the big, juicy, flavorful fried shrimp; broiled New York strip steaks served with onion rings; and local favorite sautéed chicken livers. Meals were served with choice of French fries or baked potato, hot homemade rolls and salad. The homemade bleu cheese salad dressing was celebrated for being filled with chunks of the tasty cheese. The Carriage House advertised its use of local products from Kerns Bakery, Lay's Meat Market and Selecto Meats from the East Tennessee Packing Company and JFG Coffee.

George Consin was a fascinating figure who was featured in national press before it was the trend for chefs and restaurants to be made in the media. Consin was the cover photo feature in "Who's Who in the Restaurant Business" in a restaurant association magazine, which detailed how his business grew from six employees to fifty in four years. A travel and recreation magazine for physicians later featured him in an article in which the writer had described his visit to Knoxville and dining at Consin's restaurant. A story of Consin finding a huge, inch-long and half-inch-wide pearl embedded in an oyster at the restaurant also made national news. In 1969, Knoxville hosted a Republican National Convention, and Consin was selected to serve 1,300 people, including Ronald Reagan and other political dignitaries, at a sit-down banquet in Knoxville's Civic Coliseum. He built a charcoal pit twenty feet long and four feet wide and hired ten chefs to cook steaks and get them out as quickly as possible.

Perhaps Consin's pinnacle of success occurred in 1976, when his Carriage House restaurant was named to the list of Top 400 Restaurants in the World by the organization World Famous International Restaurants. It was the first time the award had been given to a restaurant in Knoxville and ensured that the Carriage House would be listed by travel agencies, magazines and other organizations as a recommended place for travelers to visit while in the Southeast.

Over the years, Consin accumulated other interests, properties and businesses, one of which was the area franchise for the national chain of Bonanza Steak Houses. Hearing of an interested buyer from a friend, Consin called up Gene Huskey and offered to sell, even spontaneously offering to throw in the Carriage House in the deal. The two men met the following day, and the deal was made. Consin planned to, and did, become involved in community activities and civic organizations. He was elected vice chairman of the Knox County Housing Authority and also appointed on the Malpractice Review Board to serve a six-year term. But the allure of the restaurant world beckoned Consin back, and he resigned both those positions in order to return to the restaurant business.

In 1980, with hardly any promotion except for a sign out front, George Consin opened his Garden Cafeteria at 4416 Chapman Highway. I always say word of mouth is such an influence in Knoxville, and apparently the word had gotten out about Consin's project, as, after being open only two hours for lunch, he had already served 572 guests. The Garden Cafeteria was located in an old Ponderosa Steak House building that was revamped to showcase a flowing fountain in the center of the restaurant. Soft lighting and a rustic interior provided a relaxing atmosphere for Consin's guests. The cafeteria featured a choice from four or five meat and seafood entrées daily, plus a variety of soups, salads and vegetables. Bread and desserts were made from scratch by baker Betty Grove and included her German chocolate cake, carrot cake and an old-fashioned stack cake from a family recipe over one hundred years old.

So in the end, George Consin returned to his true love of the restaurant business, even though he was the first to admit, "It hasn't always been peaches and cream." Consin stated that his advice to young people was to work hard at what they enjoyed. "If what you are doing is enjoyable, it doesn't become work. It is more like play, even if you put in a twenty-hour day." When Consin retired in 1982, it was noted that he was the longest continuous restaurant operator then living in Knoxville.

But George Consin's influence didn't end there. I recently received an e-mail from a friend and longtime Knoxville resident saying their family used to enjoy eating at the Brass Rail on Gay Street. I remembered this restaurant being mentioned to me several times by local guests on my tours as one of their favorites. The Brass Rail was owned by Frank Kotsianas, who was brought to Knoxville from Greece in 1946 by his brother George Consin to work at the Garden Restaurant when he was fourteen years old. After serving in Army Intelligence during the Korean War, Kotsianas returned to Knoxville in the 1950s and, at age twenty-six, opened a restaurant of his own, called the Brass Rail, at 605 South Gay Street, right across from the Tennessee Theater.

The Brass Rail took downtown dining by storm with its delicious cuisine. Kotsianas specialized in beef such as New York strip, filet mignon and even a marinated sirloin beef kabob, skewered with hunks of onion and green pepper and garnished with pepperoncini and Greek olives over a rice pilaf. Other best-selling entrées included crispy fried shrimp, spaghetti and barbecue spareribs served with a tart and hot tomato-based sauce. An appetizer of jumbo shrimp cocktail featured huge and tender shrimp with a tangy cocktail sauce, but would you believe folks used to eat escargot in downtown Knoxville? The broiled snails were served in a garlic butter sauce at the Brass Rail. All meals were served with a choice of baked potato or French fries and a salad.

Actress Jean Simmons dined at the Brass Rail every night while filming the movie *All the Way Home* in Knoxville. The movie was based on the Pulitzer Prize–winning novel *A Death in the Family* by acclaimed Knoxville author James Agee.

By the 1960s, Kotsianas was joined by his cousin Gus Ligdis and, later, Frank Sipsis, who eventually became his equal partners in the Brass Rail, each with a third share. But understanding that the population of Knoxville was moving west, and wanting to expand, Kotsianas focused on opening a restaurant on Kingston Pike, in West Knoxville. The Ivanhoe, House of Beef, an old English-type pub, opened in 1968 at 7316 Kingston Pike (this later became Copper Cellar West and Cappuccinos). Kotsianas opened the restaurant with thirty investors. The groundbreaking for the four-hundred-seat, $500,000 restaurant was attended by Kotsianas, Mayor Leonard Rogers and Tennessee's U.S. representative, John Duncan Sr. The Ivanhoe was described as English flair meets Greek know-how.

Steak and seafood were the stars of the Ivanhoe. A glassed-in, ten-foot charcoal steak pit was built into one of the brick interior walls and was manned by a chef who would personally cook each steak to order. The steak was shipped in from Knickerbocker in New York and the Oakland Company in Chicago, then aged three weeks in a special thirty-one-degree meat room. A separate gas grill was located in the kitchen to cater to other tastes of the guests. Additional offerings included roast turkey, baked Virginia ham and roast beef, as well as an oyster bar. New Zealand lobster tails, imported red scampi, fresh crab, rainbow trout, pompano and fresh jumbo shrimp were some of the seafood specialties. Vegetables, salads and individual loaves of homemade bread rounded out the meals. One of the Ivanhoe's wonderful steak dinners for two could be had for around ten dollars in 1968.

To make sure the atmosphere of the dining room would complement the food, Kotsianas hired interior decorator Mrs. Maynard Holt to design the space, which she did in high style. The entrance, or foyer, was made to look like an eight-sided Camelot tent, with tent-striped wallpaper, a peaked ceiling and a heavy castle door. The pub was to the left. Guests entered the pub through wrought-iron gates. Holt chose a metallic armor plate wallpaper from Seabrook in New York, which sold for thirty dollars a roll. She hung an old English breastplate on black velvet on the north wall. To the right was the ladies' room, which was made to look delicate and dainty with Louis XVI court French furniture in gold and white, with gold sconces hung on the wall. Straight ahead was the huge main dining room, called the Open Hearth Room. Heavy tables with turned pedestal bases and captain's chairs trimmed in leather were handmade by Shelby-Williams of Morristown. An Ivanhoe crest was created by Holt and incorporated into a gold carpeting with black inlay by Masland and also emblazoned into custom china place settings. The Ivanhoe used gold tablecloths with red placemats. Antique crossed swords hung over the hearth. There were two rooms, called the Sirloin Room and the Knight's Stable, that could be used for private dining or opened up to create a large banquet room for business or club meetings. These rooms featured English paneling and gold banners with the Ivanhoe crest in black. Handmade, antique light fixtures completed the atmosphere of the restaurant.

By 1976, Kotsianas had sold both the Ivanhoe and the Brass Rail. The new owners of the Ivanhoe, Ted West and Robert Morris, owned Quail Creek Country Club at Cedar Springs and the Sheraton Hotel in Gatlinburg. They had big plans to change the Ivanhoe into a New Orleans–style restaurant featuring French cuisine and drinks and to build a three-hundred-unit high-rise motel with a revolving restaurant at the top on the adjoining property, which would sprawl from Kingston Pike to the Deane Hill Country Club. That project did not materialize, and the former country club and golf course became the residential Grove at Deane Hill.

Kotsianas sold his share of the Brass Rail to his business partners, Ligdis and Sipsis, who opened a second location at 8207 Kingston Pike. It was emphasized that parking was available for ninety cars, as ease of parking was a major factor that drew the population out of the downtown area. The interior was done in the style of 1977, with natural wood grain paneling; chairs and booths upholstered in gold, orange, green and yellow; and handcrafted macramé baskets filled with flowers hanging from the ceiling. Even though design trends changed with the times, the standard of quality service did not, and Ligdis and Sipsis required servers to attend special classes specific to restaurant service.

The Brass Rail downtown closed in 1976 as the 600 block of Gay Street was being redeveloped. Seven other businesses were forced to relocate or close, including the Hastee-Tastee Diner and Mr. Yogurt's Lite Food Bar. The winning proposal for the construction was submitted by the Triad Development Company. It was Triad that commissioned our famous Oarsman sculpture, which was installed on the same block in 1988.

By November 1977, the Brass Rail West had closed, and the space was taken by brothers Casey and Hassan Homasey to house their Café de Roi, which came complete with a royal theme. The focus of Café de Roi was continental cuisine. Some of the specialties included chateaubriand; lobster Thermidor; a crown rack of lamb; a roast duckling bigarade, which specifically used the Seville or "bitter" orange for its sweet glaze; a traditional Boeuf Wellington; and a beef roulade, a slice of filet rolled around a seasoned stuffing. The entrées were served on a bed of rice enhanced with raisins and almonds. Some of Café de Roi's more unusual appetizers were snails in red wine sauce and potted baby shrimp in garlic butter. Crepes made to order were offered at brunch, and Café de Roi offered a weekday lunch buffet for $1.99 in 1977. As fantastic as it sounds, Knoxville diners didn't keep Café de Roi in business.

Meanwhile, Frank Kotsianas became involved in helping bring a new dining concept into town, called Darryl's. Darryl's was part of Creative Dining Food Systems Inc., from Raleigh, North Carolina, and was owned by Darryl Davis, Charles Winston and Thad Eure Jr., all of Raleigh. The three had sketched out an idea for a pizza and burger joint on a napkin over a late-night dinner and opened their first Darryl's restaurant in 1970. The Knoxville Darryl's opened in 1979. Each Darryl's had a tag of a year that was significant to where it opened. The Knoxville Darryl's official name was Darryl's 1879, for the year the University of Tennessee was officially named the University of Tennessee.

At Darryl's, the décor was frivolous, the food was fried and the atmosphere was fun. The building looked like a big old saloon from the Wild West. "Oh, Darryl's, everyone sat in something different!" my friend exclaimed. I have to laugh reading some of the reviews, noting that at Darryl's you didn't just eat, you had to "eat cute," and the one that described the interior as a "combination garage and bordello hidden in an old barn." At Darryl's, you could eat in a double-decker bus brought in from London, an antique fire engine, a jail cell, an elevator cage or even an old Ferris wheel cart. The large, two-story dining room was outfitted with all types of antiques and "elegant junk." The focal point was an enormous crystal chandelier that had adorned the lobby of a hotel in Cincinnati. Wooden merry-go-round animals, more than one hundred functioning gas lights and a snow-white cockatoo in a large cage added to the atmosphere. The Knoxville Darryl's also featured a four-foot-tall wood Indian that had been hand carved by an artist from East Tennessee.

One cool program that Darryl's implemented was its 3-D Darryl's Designated Driver. Groups of three or more guests in the lounge could choose a non-drinking designated driver for the evening who would receive complimentary non-alcoholic drinks and a five-dollar meal coupon.

The food at Darryl's? Never mind, it was fun! Although I will mention that the most expensive menu item in 1979 was a steak, priced at $6.95. The eclectic eatery made dining entertaining and exciting and, in a way, made it OK for us to accept the influx of chain restaurants that were to come. The Darryl's franchise grew to thirty-six restaurants in nine states but in 2002 closed twenty-five of them on a single day. There is one remaining Darryl's left, in Greensboro, North Carolina, bought by William "Marty" Kotis and renamed Darryl's Wood Fired Grill. Let's go!

In 1980, Kotsianas opened London House Furnishings at the Downtown West Shopping Center. By 1986, he had become involved in a project to develop the Franklin Square Shops, at 9700 Kingston Pike, and decided to move his furniture business there. Interestingly, he also opened several gourmet food shops in the center. The Gourmet Galleria was a delicatessen featuring imported and domestic meats and cheeses, as well as twenty brands of coffee, ground to order, and a butcher counter with select cuts of beef, fresh veal and Colorado spring lamb. The European Bakery offered homemade French bread, Vienna bread, croissants, hot cross buns, Danishes, cakes, pastries and desserts. Plum Good Yogurt offered many flavors of soft yogurt with a variety of fresh tropical fruits for toppings. A specialty of the shop was Kotsianas's take on a profiterole or pâte à choux, a French puff pastry filled with a yogurt center. And wouldn't you know it, but there was a spot at Franklin Square that was just perfect for a restaurant. Kotsi's Charcoal Grill opened in 1986.

At Kotsi's, beef, ribs, lamb and poultry were cooked on an eight-foot rotisserie that slowly rotated over charcoal briquettes. The rotisserie was custom made for Kotsi's, based on a recommendation to Kotsianas by a guest who had seen one while visiting France. The lobby was designed so that guests could have a full view of the glassed-in rotisserie and grill, playing into the trend of open or visible kitchens.

In a moment of fate, celebrity chef Tim Love got his start working in restaurants at Kotsi's. Love was attending the University of Tennessee and hoping to get a job bartending. Upon applying for the job, Love told Kotsianas that he "didn't know anything about cooking." Kotsianas offered him a job making salads, which began Love's career in the food business, under the tutelage of Frank Kotsianas.

In 1991, Kotsianas sold Kotsi's for $600,000 to fellow restaurateur Mike Connor to be the first of his Chop House concept. Kotsianas had been in the restaurant business for over forty years and joked that he was almost too tired to talk. He noted that part of his philosophy for success had been putting profits back into his businesses so that they could grow and better serve customers. Kotsianas stated, in true Greek style, that "my true satisfaction is the day-to-day pursuit of excellence, excellence in food and excellence in service."

The influence of the Greek restaurateurs runs far and wide through Knoxville. Perhaps when you patronize one of our modern restaurants and notice a Greek salad, omelet or pizza on the menu, the thought of the determination of these men and families and their pursuit of excellence might bring a smile to your face.

PART V

Big Business, Tourism and the Heart of Knoxville

CHAPTER 13

THE BELOVED S&W CAFETERIA

$\mathcal{G}$f there was no more revered restaurant in Knoxville than Regas, there was no more beloved than the S&W Cafeteria. A wistful, "Oh… the S&W," is the most common response to any mention of this lost and cherished eatery.

S&W was a chain of cafeterias that began in Charlotte, North Carolina. Frank Sherrill and Fred Webber got their experience preparing food for large groups of people by serving as mess sergeants during World War I. Sherrill learned about cafeterias during a trip to California and brought the concept back home to Charlotte. In 1920, with $3,400, the duo opened the first S&W Cafeteria, the name taken from the initials of their last names. They opened S&W Cafeterias in Asheville, Chattanooga, Roanoke, Raleigh, Atlanta and Washington, D.C. Eventually, Sherrill bought out Webber, due to their differing views on being open on Sundays, but kept the name S&W and grew it to a height of twenty-seven stores. The early S&W buildings were designed in the popular Art Deco style; however, the later stores were built more in the malls and shopping centers of suburbia.

The Knoxville S&W opened in its first location in 1927, in a combination of two buildings right next to the Tennessee Theater on the 600 block of Gay Street, at a cost of $65,000. The most modern restaurant equipment available in 1927 was installed, including electric refrigeration and cooking machinery, electric conveyors and a ventilating system capable of ventilating the entire building every two minutes.

The S&W Cafeteria. *McClung Historical Collection.*

Knoxville was a very busy city, with people working, shopping and attending movies and shows downtown or "uptown," as I've heard many longtime residents declare. Many folks tell me how, even as children, they were allowed to ride the bus into town by themselves to go to a movie, shopping or lunch at the S&W.

President Franklin D. Roosevelt signed the TVA Act in 1933 as part of his New Deal to help the nation recover from the Great Depression. The Tennessee Valley Authority soon found its headquarters and home in Knoxville and became a great aid to the region in terms of establishing flood control and navigation of the Tennessee River, providing for reforestation and agricultural improvement and generating energy and electricity for industrial development. The TVA's thousands of employees were also a boon to business in downtown Knoxville, especially for restaurants like the S&W.

The S&W moved to its new location at 516 South Gay Street in 1937. The site was composed of three buildings merged into one. During this time of the Depression, labor and materials were cheap, and the finest details could be incorporated into the S&W. The new Art Deco palace had a sleek exterior of terra cotta, bronze and Virolite structural glass, and revolving doors ushered guests into its elegant dining room with polished terrazzo floors. A Hammond B3 organ was located near the staircase, where guests would often be entertained by the S&W house organist, Lois Harris. Eighteen- by twenty-two-foot Rosadora mirrors lined the walls of each side of the lobby, and a veneer of seven different woods— zebrawood, walnut, lacewood, aspen, bur, myrtle and primavera—made up the paneling. The ceiling was adorned with thick crown molding and plaster and metal ornamental medallions, each weighing about two hundred pounds. Marble and granite were used throughout the building, and the grand stairway led to the mezzanine, where the walls were covered in approximately 9,500 capiz shells. Banquet rooms were available on the third floor. The kitchen was located in the basement, and food would be brought up by a dumbwaiter, then a second dumbwaiter would carry dirty dishes back down to the washing area.

Like many of the downtown restaurants of the time, the S&W served breakfast. In the late 1940s, breakfast might include two eggs any style for twenty cents, Canadian bacon or country sausage for fifteen cents, a strip of bacon for eight cents or two for fifteen cents, fried potatoes for ten cents, salt mackerel for twenty-five cents and glazed apples or oatmeal for ten cents. A daily S&W special lunch plate might have consisted of a beef hash "pattie," slicked dill pickle, au gratin potatoes, buttered new peas and hot rolls and butter for thirty cents. Coffee and tea were five cents, with free refills. "Noon Suggestions" were composed of comfort favorites such as roast prime rib of beef, fried filet of haddock, baked spaghetti, beef steak pie, deviled fresh crab and a braised pork chop with fruit, along with Salisbury steak, meatloaf, bone-in ham, fried chicken, fried salmon trout, smothered half spring chicken, broiled tenderloin steak and even chicken chop suey with rice. Local favorite liver and onions or liver and bacon and even Depression-era staples such as cow tongue, pig brains and pork knuckles with sauerkraut were available. Sides included nearly every type of vegetable, such as black-eyed peas, mashed turnips, creamed potatoes, lima beans, kale greens, string beans, collard greens, fried eggplant or okra, green peas, whole kernel corn, pinto beans, hominy, stewed tomatoes, oven roasted potatoes and an intriguing yellow rice. Desired desserts were custard, chess and coconut cream pies, bread pudding and a special graham cracker concoction with pineapple icing. Thursday nights were "Family Night," and a family meal with all the trimmings could be had for twenty-five cents. Movies for the kids were shown on the mezzanine on Family Night.

Frank Sherrill's idea was to "sell a lot of good food at a price people can pay." This philosophy seemed to work well for quality-minded Knoxvillians, as the S&W became an extremely popular restaurant and would serve up to 700 customers an hour, up to two thousand meals a day. The population often stood in lines that extended the length of the building and also onto the sidewalk. A staff of 250 was required to operate the restaurant. But by the late 1970s, business began dwindling as the majority of the population began to move to the west side of town. After a fifty-four-year run, the S&W closed in 1981.

A favorite server at the S&W was Tennyson "Slim" Dickson, who worked there for fifty-two years, from 1929, two years after it opened, until 1981. Slim was a tall, slender black man who always dressed for service in a black suit, white shirt and black bow tie. This industrious man with a third-grade education arrived in Knoxville by bus from Greeneville. He had told the bus driver he didn't have any money to pay for the ride but that he had a bag with him that the driver could keep until he brought the money to pay him. Besides some personal belongings, Slim also had a pistol in the bag. He went to the back of the bus, took out the pistol and then handed the bag over to the driver. When they arrived in Knoxville, Slim pawned the pistol and returned and paid for the bus ride.

Guests at the S&W loved Slim, and he loved them. He became very skilled in hospitality—greeting guests and providing for their every need. Slim knew and called many guests by their first name and could bring a smile to the face of anyone who wasn't having the best day. He was also known as incredibly personable, generous and giving. Some called him "a jewel of a man."

In his free time, Slim took odd jobs, such as year-round yard work, moving furniture, washing windows, vacuuming, mopping and house cleaning. Slim said he worked for his health, to keep active and for a clear mind and clean thoughts. Probably not many would guess that the unassuming Slim used his earnings to purchase real estate, at one time owning thirty-five houses in East Knoxville.

Slim said he cried the day the S&W Cafeteria closed and that people called him for days and days and told him they saw him crying on TV about the closing and that they cried right along with him. He also said at the end of his journey that he hoped he would meet all his former guests again in heaven. I have a feeling they were overjoyed to see him.

As the S&W building sat empty, the city tried to decide what to do with it. No one wanted the treasured building destroyed. An award-winning architect noted the S&W as one of the three or four finest buildings of Knoxville. Other local architects agreed that if the building were lost, nothing even comparable could be built to take its place. Various plans had been presented to put the building to use, including a transit center, a health club and the Justice Center, but none ever worked out. By 1995, an arrangement came about for the S&W building to be demolished to make way for the Regal Entertainment Group's new eight-screen movie theater, the Regal Riviera.

Knox Heritage jumped into action again and requested aid from Mayor Bill Haslam, who had been a big proponent of the new theater to boost redevelopment of downtown, with providing a time delay in order for the organization to produce an alternate plan to preserve the S&W building. Architect Faris Eid created a sketch of the proposed movie theater that would allow the S&W building to stay intact. Fortunately, the Regal group agreed to the new design. The new movie theater was built, and the S&W building remained.

In 2009, following a $4.5 million restoration, the S&W Grand opened in the space. It was not a cafeteria but a very nice full-service restaurant. In January 2011, the S&W Grand unexpectedly closed.

By June 2011, a new tenant had moved into the S&W building, a Michigan-based beauty school and salon, Douglas J Companies. In a bold move, all the restaurant equipment was auctioned off, and the building was overhauled to accommodate the salon. An Aveda retail store and salon space took over the ground floor. The bar became shampoo stations, while the kitchen was turned into treatment rooms for facials, body treatments and waxing. The top floor, which held the banquet rooms, became a manicure, pedicure and hair-cutting station. Classrooms were created in the adjoining building.

To be sure, the S&W Cafeteria created many beautiful memories for Knoxvillians, and beauty is still being created at the iconic S&W building.

CHAPTER 14

HAROLD AND ADDIE'S KOSHER-STYLE FOOD CENTER

H ard work," stated Addie Shersky. "And lots of it," added her husband, Harold. That was the recipe for success at Harold's Kosher-Style Food Center, or Harold's Deli. Harold was born in Knoxville on East Vine Avenue. He served in World War II and met Addie while visiting a relative in Louisville, Kentucky. Harold and Addie married and began their lives together in 1941. They began their career in food together in 1948, when Harold quit his job as a shoe salesman at Castle Shoes on Gay Street and bought a Jewish grocery and deli from O.B. Seagall. Harold and Addie had a long and successful run in marriage and, despite having no previous experience in the food industry, much success in business.

The building location of Harold's Deli at 131 South Gay Street was part of the Gay Street viaduct project of 1919. In hilly Knoxville, horses pulling wagons of freight from the railroad up into town were under such stress that sometimes sparks could be seen shooting out from their horseshoes. The viaducts were built to make travel easier up the massive hill. The construction of the viaducts raised the level of the 100 block of Gay Street up to twelve feet in some places and created levels of basement space where buildings and shops had once existed. This created the fabled "Underground Knoxville" that so many of my tour guests have heard of and inquire about. Yes, Virginia, there is an Underground Knoxville, and it runs the entire length of the 100 block of Gay Street.

In the early 1920s, the 100 block was a highly desired area for business. The area was filled with successful businesses, and it was almost impossible to obtain property on the block. Harold and Addie remembered when the sidewalks were so busy you could hardly put a foot down and the streets were so busy you could hardly cross for all the traffic.

In addition to the other businesses on the block, by the late 1930s, WNOX had moved its *Mid-Day Merry-Go-Round* live radio show to the 100 block, where it drew a huge crowd. The show had been such a hit at the Market House that it soon had to be moved to a larger space in the top of the Andrew Johnson Hotel at 912 South Gay Street. The *Mid-Day Merry-Go-Round* shows continued to grow, and the audience would sometimes rise to one thousand people. The crowd size so taxed the elevators in the hotel that WNOX was asked to find another space.

The *Mid-Day Merry-Go-Round* found a new home at a building with a six-hundred-seat auditorium adjacent to the Sterchi Brothers Furniture Company at 116 South Gay Street and, in fact, was sponsored by Sterchi Brothers Furniture. Sterchi Brothers was one of the South's main suppliers of phonographs and records. It began promoting and recording local "hillbilly" musicians in order to boost sales. For some time, sales averaged seventy-five thousand records per month in its twenty-six stores. Stars from the show such as June Carter Cash, Don Gibson, Lester Flatt and Earl Scruggs, Chet Atkins, Archie Campbell and many more frequented the restaurants on the 100 block, including Harold's and the Three Feathers Café.

Harold's brother Leonard Shersky operated the Three Feathers Café, just a few doors down, at 101 South Gay Street. The Three Feathers was a sandwich shop and beer joint frequented by talented singer, songwriter and performer Arthur Q. Smith. Smith was a hard-drinking alcoholic who would sometimes write and sell a song for fifteen or twenty-five dollars, or even the price of his bar tab. Unfortunately, some performers took advantage of Smith's illness and procured songs from him for a pittance and went on to have hits with them that Arthur never received royalties from. Arthur Q. was a bit in on the act, however, stating that folks didn't know how many times he had actually sold those songs.

The Three Feathers Café closed in 1952, but Harold's continued on. In 1955, WNOX moved from its Gay Street location to a new building at the old Whittle Springs Resort, with plans to have a television station. When the country music stars stopped coming to downtown Knoxville, and to Harold's, plenty of locals still came—city councilmen, politicians, businessmen, lawyers, professors, journalists. Although they ran a Jewish deli, people from all backgrounds and walks of life frequented Harold and Addie's eatery.

The Sherskys were once featured in *Southern Living* magazine, but Harold and Addie didn't seek out publicity; it just naturally came to them because of their high-traffic location and the eclectic mix of their customer base. They were noted as down-to-earth, highly respected people. A longtime employee stated that Harold and Addie were more like a brother and sister to her than bosses and that they would never do anything that wasn't just right. Addie was described as extremely kind and would make the rounds of the dining room to check on customers—not particularly on their food, which she left in confidence with Harold and their longtime cooks and servers, but on their lives in general. Addie and Harold were in tune with their customers and their needs, and guests noted that they never felt rushed to leave Harold's. "You just try to be nice to people," Harold explained. "Everybody's special. We treat them all alike. We're from the old school. We still believe in the Golden Rule."

"Oh, we would go to Harold's, it was so exotic…It was a Jewish delicatessen!" one acquaintance exclaimed. What were folks eating at Harold's? Breakfast began at 6:00 a.m. and might include kosher beef bacon, salami or bologna with eggs, a lox platter with bagel or cheese blintzes. Lunch might start with herring in wine sauce or cream with bread

Harold's Deli menu. *McClung Historical Collection.*

APPETIZERS - JUICES

HERRING IN WINE SAUCE OR CREAM - Bread & Butter	3.55
CHOPPED LIVER, ONIONS & GARNISH - Bread & Butter	4.45
HOT POTATO KNISH	1.35
With Sour Cream	1.85
JUICES - Orange, Tomato, Grapefruit	.65 1.20

SOUPS - CHILI

SOUP OF THE DAY - Served With Crackers	2.15
MATZO BALL SOUP (Tuesday, Friday & Saturday) Served With Crackers	2.65
CHILI & BEANS - Served With Crackers	2.45
Bread & Butter Add .50	

SALADS – FISH PLATTERS

Served With Lettuce, Tomato, Onion
Dill Pickle, Potato Salad Off Slaw & A Bagel

TUNA FISH SALAD	5.45
CHOPPED LIVER	6.65
WHITE FISH SALAD	6.65
INDIVIDUAL TIN WHITE MEAT TUNA	5.45
CHUNKY CHICKEN SALAD	5.45
IMPORTED SARDINES	5.45
SAM'S TUNA (Individual Tin White Meat Tuna Mixed with Light Mayonnaise Pickle Relish & Onion)	6.45

NOVA LOX

Served With Greek Olives, Cream Cheese, Swiss Cheese,
Lettuce, Tomato, Onion & A Bagel 7.45

CHEF'S SALAD - Breast of Turkey, Swiss Cheese, Egg Slices, Lettuce, Tomato, Dill Pickle - Choice of Dressing Served With Crackers	5.45
HEALTH SALAD - Scoop of Cottage Cheese, Hard-Boiled Egg, Lettuce, Tomato, Dill Pickle - Served With Crackers	4.15
TOSSED SALAD - Choice of Dressing, Crackers	1.95

DAIRY DISHES

CHEESE BLINTZES with Sour Cream & Jelly	(3) 4.45 (2) 3.45
Fruit Topping OR Applesauce	Add .85
BOWL OF COTTAGE CHEESE - Sour Cream, Bread & Butter	2.95
CHILLED BEET BORSCHT & SOUR CREAM - Bread & Butter	2.95
BOWL OF BOILED POTATOES & SOUR CREAM – Bread & Butter	3.35

SIDE ORDERS

POTATO SALAD	1.15
COLE SLAW	1.15
BAKED VEGETARIAN BEANS	1.25
KOSHER DILL PICKLE	.75
KOSHER DILL TOMATO	.75
GREEK OLIVES	1.15
ITALIAN PEPPERONCINI	1.15
POTATO KNISH	1.35
With Sour Cream	1.85
CREAM CHEESE	.55
COTTAGE CHEESE	1.15
APPLESAUCE	1.15
SOUR CREAM	1.25
HOT VEGETABLE	1.15
SLICED TOMATO & ONIONS	1.55
JALAPENO DILL PICKLE CHIPS	.75

SANDWICH SPECIALTIES

Served Hot or Cold
With Dill Pickle & Peppers

REUBEN – Corned Beef, Swiss Cheese Topped with Fresh Barrel Kraut On Long Light or Dark Roll, Russian Dressing	4.95
GILBERT – Roast Beef, Breast of Turkey on Long Light or Dark Roll, Lettuce, Russian Dressing	5.15
GIANT TWIST – Corned Beef, Turkey, Salami, Swiss Cheese, Russian Dressing On An Egg Twist Roll – Potato Salad OR Slaw	7.25
BREAST OF TURKEY & SMOKEY CHEDDAR CHEESE On Long Light or Dark Roll, Lettuce, Mayonnaise	4.15
HAROLD'S SAMPLER – 3 ON A PLATE – 3 Sandwiches on Mini Onion Rolls With Potato Salad OR Slaw, Dill Pickle, Corned Beef, Turkey, Chopped Liver OR Your Choices	7.25
HOT PASTRAMI, KNACKWURST, IMPORTED SWISS On Long Light or Dark Roll	6.15
TURKEY SPECIAL – Breast of Turkey, Lettuce, Russian Dressing On Seeded Bun, Potato Salad OR Slaw	4.95
ROAST BEEF SPECIAL – On Seeded Bun, Lettuce, Russian Dressing, Potato Salad, OR Slaw	4.95
HOT PASTRAMI SPECIAL – On Large Onion Roll, Potato Salad OR Slaw	4.95
HOAGIE – Salami, Imported Swiss Cheese, Lettuce, Tomato, Onion	3.75
CORNED BEEF OR PEPPERED BEEF HOAGIE – With Imported Swiss Cheese, Lettuce, Tomato, Onion on Long Light or Dark Roll	4.95
PEPPERED BEEF & CREAM CHEESE – On Long Light or Dark Roll	4.15
TRIPLE CHEESE – Your Choices On Long Light or Dark Roll, Lettuce, Tomato, Mayonnaise	4.15
CHOPPED STEAK – On Seeded Bun, Lettuce, Tomato, Onion, Potato Salad OR Slaw	4.25

NOVA LOX & CREAM CHEESE

On Toasted Bagel, Dill Pickle
Sliced Onions If Your Prefer 4.45

HOT & COLD SPECIALTIES

CORNED BEEF & PASTRAMI PLATTER With Side Order, Dill Pickle, Bread & Butter	10.95
Extra Side Order & Bread (Serves 2)	11.95
KNACKWURST With Side Order, Dill Pickle, Bread & Butter (2) 5.95	(1) 3.95
TWO FRANKFURTERS With Side Order, Dill Pickle, Bread & Butter	4.45
HOT ROAST BEEF SANDWICH With Potatoes, Brown Gravy, Dill Pickle	5.15
CHILI SPECIAL – Bowl of Chili and Frankfurter On A Bun, Dill Pickle	3.95
ASSORTED COLD MEATS PLATTER – Your Choice of Any 4 Cold Meats OR 3 Meats & 2 Cheeses With Side Order, Dill Pickle, Bread & Butter	10.95
Extra Side Order & Bread (Serves 2)	11.95

SIDE ORDERS – POTATO SALAD, SLAW, BAKED BEANS,
FRESH BARREL KRAUT

DELI SANDWICHES

Served Hot Or Cold On Rye, Whole, Wheat Or Pumpernickel Bread,
Rolls, Seeded Buns, Onion Rolls, Bagels,
Dill Pickle Slices, Peppers

	Regular	Double
CORNED BEEF	3.70	6.70
EXTRA LEAN CORNED BEEF	4.70	7.70
PASTRAMI	3.70	6.70
EXTRA LEAN PASTRAMI	4.70	7.70
PEPPERED BEEF	3.70	6.70
LIVERWURST	3.70	6.70
BEEF TONGUE	5.15	8.15
BREAST OF TURKEY	3.70	6.70
ROAST BEEF	3.70	6.70
ROAST BEEF BRISKET	4.70	7.70
SALAMI OR BOLOGNA	3.60	6.60
KNACKWURST ON BUN	2.95	----
FRANKFURTER ON BUN	1.65	----
TUNA SALAD, LETTUCE, TOMATO	3.55	5.95
CHOPPED LIVER, LETTUCE, TOMATO	4.15	7.15
CHUNKY CHICKEN SALAD, LETT., TOM.	3.95	6.35
CREAM CHEESE ON BAGEL	1.75	----
CHEESE, LETTUCE, TOMATO – Your Choice of Imported Swiss, Smoked Cheddar, Cheddar, Sharp, Muenster, Hot Pepper, Mozzarella, Provolone		3.15

Slice OR Kraut On Sandwich Add .50
Any Cheese On Sandwich Add .50
Lettuce And Tomato Add .40
Onion, No Charge

BEVERAGES

COFFEE, TEA, MILK
BREWED DECAF, HOT CHOCOLATE

DR. BROWN'S SODAS - CREAM DIET CREAM, BLACK CHERRY, DIET BLACK
CHERRY, GINGER ALE, ROOT BEER, CELRAY

COCA COLA, DIET COKE, SPRITE

DOMESTIC & IMPORTED BEERS

DESSERTS

CREAM CHEESE CAKE	2.35
With Fruit Topping	2.95
PINEAPPLE NUT PIE	2.35
CARROT CAKE	2.35
APPLE PIE	1.75
With Ice Cream	2.35
VANILLA ICE CREAM	1.25

Harold's Deli menu. *McClung Historical Collection.*

and butter, chopped liver with onions or a hot potato knish with sour cream. Chilled beet borscht was a specialty, as were salads of tuna, white fish or sardines. How about a kosher dill pickle, dill tomato or jalapeño dill pickle chips? Matzo ball soup was a daily special, along with corned beef and cabbage, spaghetti with meat sauce and chopped sirloin steak. And then of course the sandwiches—pastrami, peppered beef, liverwurst, beef tongue, knackwurst, hot roast beef or a Reuben on pumpernickel. Oh, you thought those cute little sliders you like so much were created in our modern restaurants? Harold included them on his Harold's Sampler— corned beef, turkey and chopped liver on three mini onion rolls served with potato salad or slaw and a dill pickle. Addie did most of the baking and served up desserts of pineapple nut pie, carrot cake, cheesecake or hot apple pie.

In 1986, Harold's was averaging 125 guests per day, with typical checks of four dollars per person. What did he attribute the success of his deli to? "You just open the door in the morning and hope for the best."

In 2003, Addie passed away after a long battle with cancer. Harold continued on until 2005, when he was injured in a car accident and forced to take time to recuperate. Harold enlisted the help of Chef Bruce Bogartz, who by this time was running his namesake restaurant, Bogartz, in the Homberg area. The two had known each other for years, and Shersky had even been mentioning the idea of him taking over the deli to Bogartz since 1989, when the talented chef graduated from culinary school in Philadelphia. The partnership was short-lived, with Bogartz leaving after three months, citing financial pressures in the business. Shortly afterward, Harold's closed for good.

Harry's. *Cahets.*

Harold passed away in 2008 without seeing the next incarnation of the building. In 2010, Ben and Amy Becker opened Harry's. The coincidental name was not for Harold Shersky but for their two-year-old son, Harry Becker. The Beckers had both attended the New England Culinary Institute in Vermont. They were Jewish but opted to open a Jewish-Italian deli that served classic Jewish cuisine but also added pork products such as bacon and prosciutto. Harold and Addie had introduced Knoxville to bagels, but the Beckers introduced Knoxville to bialys—baked but not boiled, with a slight depression in the middle rather than a hole—as well as the Jewish pastry rugelach. The Beckers were on the forefront of the farm-to-table movement returning to Knoxville and marketed that they made everything they served in house. This was another example of a business being ahead of its time. Within a year, the Beckers had closed Harry's.

Unlike the Sherskys when they started out, both Bogartz and the Beckers had much previous training and experience in the food business. But as entrepreneur Greg White observed, "Harold's is not Harold's without Harold." When White was opening his innovative Nama sushi restaurant at its first tiny location, two doors down from Harold's, at 135 South Gay Street, his biggest fan was Harold Shersky. Harold Shersky, true to form, had taken an interest in his life.

In 2013, Matt Gallaher opened Knox Mason in the space, focusing on the trend of the resurgence of Appalachian foothills cuisine made nationally famous by the nearby luxury resort Blackberry Farm. Gallaher had previously worked as chef for former Knoxville mayor, who became Tennessee governor, Bill Haslam. Gallaher received an early food education from his mother, Rebecca Williams, who, I was surprised to learn, operated Miss Emily's Tea Room in Morristown and then later in Jefferson City. A lovely meal at Miss Emily's, just down the street from Carson Newman College, with my own mother and grandmother still lingers in my mind.

CHAPTER 15

TRAVELERS, LUNCH COUNTERS, SIT-INS AND DESEGREGATION

By 1944, Franklin D. Roosevelt was focused on East Tennessee again as the Great Smoky Mountains National Park was being created. Logging and clear-cutting of the late 1800s began to destroy the beauty of the area, and locals and visitors joined together in an effort to preserve the land. John D. Rockefeller donated $5 million and the United States government added $2 million, and the tracts of land were assembled to form the park. The 500,000-acre wonder is now the nation's most visited national park.

FDR and other officials and dignitaries stayed at the Andrew Johnson Hotel in Knoxville as the park was being established. The kitchen at the Andrew Johnson packed a "sumptuous southern picnic lunch" for the entourage for the trip to the mountains to tour the park, which included caviar and cheese sandwiches, fried chicken, crab salad, sardines, crackers, fruit and several kinds of bottled soft drinks.

Motorists across the country were ready to travel and explore the Great Smoky Mountains, the American South and the popular tourist destinations of Florida and the coast. Knoxville became a frequent stopping point for many travelers, as it was at the junction of Dixie Highway, U.S. 70 and Lee Highway, U.S. 11, a halfway point for many vacationers. Restaurants and tourist court motels sprang up all along Kingston Pike and Chapman Highway.

The Alhambra Tourist Court at 4249 Kingston Pike was run by George Fooshee and recommended by famed traveling salesman and author Duncan Hines. Terrace View Court, at 6400 Kingston Pike, was owned by

Alhambra Court. *Dexter Press.*

Fooshee's brother Leon and was situated at the top of Bearden hill, where "there is always a cool breeze." Each room was said to have a view of Mount LeConte and the majestic Smoky Mountains and featured fine furnishings from Sterchi Brothers Furniture Company.

Highland Grill was recommended by AAA and featured steaks along with the southern staples of fried chicken and country ham. The Dwarf Restaurant advertised local French Broad milk and ice cream, a chicken and dumplings dinner or "French fried ocean catfish" dinner for one dollar, while the Dixieland Drive-In offered a specialty called Chicken in the Rough, the world's most famous chicken dish of the time, according to *National Restaurant* magazine.

Chicken in the Rough was one of the earliest food franchises, developed by Beverly and Rubye Osborne in 1936 while on a road trip themselves. Beverly spilled their picnic basket full of fried chicken when Rubye hit a bump driving through the Oklahoma prairie, and they declared it was truly "chicken in the rough." The dish Chicken in the Rough consisted of half of a golden fried chicken, heaps of shoestring potatoes, hot buttered rolls and a jug of honey. The chicken was specifically served unjointed, without silverware and in aluminum containers that would keep the chicken hot for hours. The Dixieland Drive-In became the fourth-largest purveyor of Chicken in the Rough in the country. Special machinery was designed that could simultaneously fry and steam the chicken.

Highlands Grill. *Standard Souvenirs.*

The Dwarf Restaurant. *Manning Graphic Arts.*

Dixieland Drive-In. *Fullcolor Post Cards.*

One of the most unusual eateries of the time was the Inferno Drive-In, which was first opened on Blount Avenue, between the Henley and Gay Street bridges. The original Inferno was very small and only had a half dozen bar stools. It reportedly had a red neon light out front that formed a devil, horns, a pitchfork, blazes and a jiggling fire. The Inferno was the home of the "devil dog," a hot dog covered with a special chili. It was later moved to 2819 Chapman Highway, on the way to the Smokies. Keeping with the theme, the Inferno provided matchbooks to customers with the phrase "Go to the devil" printed on them.

Although travelers were on their way to some of the most beautiful spots in the country, in 1947 travel writer John Gunther noted that Knoxville was the "ugliest city I ever saw in America" in his book *Inside USA*. After one of my tour groups asked me to relate that story, we all burst out laughing, as of course now Knoxville constantly receives compliments on its natural beauty and cleanliness. One can't help but wonder if Gunther's sour disposition was caused by his discovery that Knoxville served beer no stronger than 3.6 percent alcohol and that the taprooms closed at 9:30 p.m.

While folks in this area would naturally do this anyway, in 1952 locals were encouraged to be kind to tourists through a Courtesy Campaign, which was accompanied by a contest created by the Knoxville Tourist Bureau and

The Inferno Drive-In. *Standard Souvenirs.*

promoted by the local newspapers. The week of August 17, 1952, C.B. Alexander, superintendent of the Oliver King Sand and Lime Company, received a cash prize of twenty-five dollars from the Dempster Brothers Company for being the most courteous person in Knoxville. Even the person nominating the recipient received an award. Alan Cruze received six Arrow shirts from J.S. Hall for nominating Alexander for always directing tourists who accidentally turned into the sand company on their right way. He noted one particular incident when a couple from Florida turned into the sand company, quite a bit away from their destination of the Alhambra Tourist Court. Alexander politely gave them directions and then encouraged them to come back again someday. Other prizes offered during the courtesy contest included an electric clock radio from Kimball's, a six-month pass for two to the Tennessee Theater and an RCA table model radio from Woodruff's.

Despite Gunther's blatant insult, tourism in Knoxville continued to grow, even as the rest of the country was reporting a decline. In 1954, Knoxville reported its biggest numbers up to then of tourist trade. That year, 1,326,611 out-of-state tourists came through the area, while 1,200,268 Tennesseans from across the state visited. The majority of tourist dollars were spent on food, with total food spending at $9,717,956.

Gunther's unpleasant remarks also prompted the Knoxville Garden Club to establish the Dogwood Driving Trails in 1955. There are now trails in all parts of the city, and our Dogwood Arts Festival hosts arts and cultural

McKee Motel/Glass House Restaurant. *Manning Graphic Arts.*

Sterchi Brothers Furniture Café. *McClung Historical Collection.*

events all through the month of April, encouraging folks to come and enjoy the beauty of Knoxville.

Meanwhile, downtown Knoxville continued to thrive. Folks often wanted a fast, convenient lunch while in town doing errands or shopping, which gave way to the rise and popularity of lunch counters. Pharmacies and department stores such as Walgreens, Woolworth's, Kress, Miller's, Rich's and even Sterchi Brothers Furniture Company provided lunch counters for their many customers.

A quick meal at a lunch counter might include cold, toasted or grilled sandwiches. BLTs, burgers, patty melts, hot dogs, club sandwiches, bacon and egg sandwiches, grilled cheese or grilled ham and cheese sandwiches with fries or onion rings were typical menu items. Soups, salads with cottage cheese, tuna salad–stuffed tomatoes, egg or chicken salads were lighter fare. Desserts were specialties of fruit or cream pies, ice cream sundaes, banana splits, floats, sodas, milkshakes and malts. Miller's Laurel Room was particularly known for its soft and airy fresh coconut cake with lemon cheese icing and Chef Henry's Heavenly Hash, a gelatin salad.

Kress lunch counter. *McClung Historical Collection.*

Kress Building. *McClung Historical Collection.*

A favorite dessert at the Knoxville Kress was the fruit and nut pudding. The recipe request amused the kitchen staff at Kress, who let the secret out that the famous fruit and nut pudding, in the true Appalachian style of using what was available, was made from day-old doughnuts or stale cake and leftover fruit pies. The recipe is as follows:

> Save up stale cake or doughnuts, fruit pies and the juice from 1 can of peaches in an empty whipped topping container in the freezer until the container is full. Combine contents of container with one 10-ounce package of frozen strawberries and perhaps a crumbled slice of bread. Add 1 teaspoon almond flavoring. Optionally add nuts or red food coloring.
>
> Heat the mixture in the saucepan, then spoon into a serving dish. Top with a hard sauce or whipped cream.

Early in 1960, segregation was being challenged by sit-ins at lunch counters. After the first sit-in occurred in February in Greensboro, North

Carolina, word spread quickly, and a group of Knoxville College students organized to conduct their own sit-in at one of Knoxville's lunch counters. The college's president convinced the students to wait until he had a chance to talk with city leaders, hoping to avoid the violence of protests occurring in other cities. Knoxville's mayor even went so far as to take a delegation of himself, two chamber of commerce officials and two Knoxville College students to attempt to meet and negotiate with chain store executives in New York to desegregate their lunch counters in Knoxville. They were unable to obtain a meeting, and the Knoxville protests began in June. Some of the Knoxville sit-in experience is documented in Merrill Proudfoot's book *Diary of a Sit-In*.

In 1963, the Committee for Orderly Desegregation of Public Facilities in Knoxville and a committee of the Knoxville Restaurant Association formed an agreement for restaurants to desegregate in Knoxville on July 5. Thirty-two local restaurants participated, including Regas, the S&W Cafeteria, the Rathskeller, Pero's, Louis', Wright's Cafeteria, the Tic-Toc Room and Helma's.

Helma's was located on the Asheville Highway, at the junction of 11E and 25W, about twelve miles east of downtown Knoxville. Helma Gilreath began her eatery in 1949 in a so-called truck stop style with two tables and six stools. She eventually established a country-style buffet that was so successful that she was able to expand to a dining room that accommodated 125 plus banquet rooms for 330. Helma once catered a meal for 5,300 employees of the local Magnavox manufacturing plant and also provided catering for the movie *All the Way Home* for scenes shot in the Smoky Mountains. A flavor of locally produced Kay's Ice Cream was patterned after Helma's famous banana pudding, and in 1985, she appeared in the pilot of an early reality show of a television series called *Wish You Were Here*, featuring *Hee Haw* variety show favorite Kenny Price. The premise of the show was that Price and his wife would travel the country in an RV and take viewers on a tour of various campgrounds and other places of interest. Helma was named Tennessee's Outstanding Restaurateur of the Year by the Tennessee Restaurant Association in 1977.

Helma was one of the committee members who attended every Restaurant Association meeting and stated that segregation in restaurants should be addressed. Everyone agreed that it should not be a problem, as East Tennessee was not as racially divided as other cities of the deeper South. When the first black patrons pulled up at Helma's, a nervous server asked, "What do we do, what do we do?" Helma calmly replied, "What do you normally do when we have customers?" The following year, President Lyndon Johnson signed the Civil Rights Act of 1964, which banned racial discrimination in voting, employment and use of public facilities. Helma's daughter related how, several years later, in the mid-1970s, University of Tennessee basketball great Bernard King came in to eat at Helma's, and many of the white men argued over who would get to buy his lunch. Knoxville, and the country, had come a long way.

PART VI

Knoxville Looks Westward, in Location and Inspiration

CHAPTER 16

THE UNIVERSITY OF TENNESSEE'S STRIP

O⟩h, you better!" my friend exclaimed about including eateries on "The Strip," the stretch of retail shops, bars and restaurants along Cumberland Avenue that runs through the University of Tennessee. The Strip has been an important part of college life for generations of Volunteers. Many viewed The Strip as a place to enjoy different eating options other than the school cafeteria. Years ago, home-style meals, rather than fast-food franchises, were the norm on The Strip.

The Strip's nickname fully revealed itself when the phenomenon of streaking on college campuses was happening all across the country. In 1974, an estimated five thousand people turned out to "streak The Strip" in Knoxville, prompting CBS news anchor Walter Cronkite, "the most trusted man in America," to name Knoxville the Streaking Capital of the World.

A long-standing tradition began on The Strip at 2204 Cumberland Avenue when Raymond Brown opened Brownie's Grill in 1939. Brownie's was the originator of another signature dish of Knoxville, Metts and Beans. Mettwurst is a German sausage made from smoked and cured minced pork. For Metts and Beans, the mettwurst is served on top of a bowl of white beans and accompanied by coleslaw, raw onions and slices of pumpernickel bread. Brownie's version topped the mettwurst with chili beans, but modern versions might top it with sauerkraut, also adding pickle relish and horseradish as accompaniments.

Raymond operated Brownie's for thirty-one years until his death in 1970. His widow, Vera, continued to run the business until the mid-'70s. Brownie's was sold and became the Old College Inn, which established as much of a long-term iconic presence as its predecessor. Jim England was one of the operators of the Old College Inn. He also owned several other businesses on The Strip, including Dugout Doug's Record Store and England Sound, which was a record and stereo store with a recording studio in the back. England went on to open the Last Lap and the University Club on The Strip before moving to Gatlinburg, where he purchased Howard's Restaurant.

As at other establishments on The Strip, the Old College Inn served another Knoxville signature item: the steamed sandwich. Steamed sandwiches became popular here in true early Appalachian style, by folks figuring out a way to use, make edible and not waste slightly old or stale bread. In the way the English and French created bread pudding, East Tennesseans made steamed sandwiches. Even though fresh bread is readily available in Knoxville these days, it's always a slight thrill to still find a steamed sandwich on a menu.

The Old College Inn was later owned by Mike Clark, who said that for many years he had operated the Old College Inn without making a profit. Clark noted that students no longer seemed to display loyalty to favorite bars or restaurants but discarded them for the next big trend. The decline in business resulted in failure to make payments on a bank note. Looking for assets to claim, in an unusual move, First National Bank wanted the name Old College Inn along with equipment as part of the payment. The bank viewed the name of the iconic eatery as an extremely valuable asset for its good, established reputation and customer brand recognition. In the end, Clark gave up the name and the location and moved to 1824 Cumberland to open the Goal Post Tavern.

Another long-standing tradition on The Strip was the Varsity Inn, which was run by Gus Kampas from 1963 to 1991. Kampas was a Greek immigrant who came to the United States at age thirteen. The Varsity Inn served breakfast, lunch and dinner and was known for burgers, hot dogs and hot roast beef. Kampas noted that restaurant business on The Strip was very good, and "it was like a football game every day" up until the 1970s, when the University of Tennessee required mandatory meal plans for students who lived in the residence halls. Kampas also noted the new tendency of everyone being in a hurry and wanting to go through a drive-through.

Eateries were also on the streets surrounding Cumberland Avenue. Byerley's Cafeteria at White Avenue and Sixteenth Street had a long run from 1944 until 1976. It was owned by Luther Byerley and was the site of some of the civil rights sit-ins before the first black students were admitted to the University of Tennessee in January 1961. Byerley had also run Uneeta Dairy Lunch on Clinch Avenue in 1919 and opened a coffee shop on Cumberland in 1928.

"There was a place where you could walk up to a trolley and get a burger," a friend remembered. That would have been Ollie's Trolley. In 1973, a trolley unit that had been brought from Louisville, Kentucky, was set up at 417 Clinch Avenue, with plans for ten more units in the Knoxville area. The concept was developed in the 1930s by Ollie Gleichenhaus, who created a special blend of seasonings for his Ollie burgers and fries. Gleichenhaus took his burgers seriously. According to Ollie, burgers were to be cooked medium rare, and if anyone ordered anything different, he would throw them out of his restaurant while using profanity.

Renee and her husband, Sameer Jubran, opened the Falafel Hut at 611 West Fifteenth Street in 1982 after being prompted by their daughter's and nephew's friends, University of Tennessee students, who came to their home occasionally to eat. The Jubrans had moved to the Knoxville area from Detroit after Sameer lost his grocery store to looters in the 1967 riots and he was shot in his second store. They chose East Tennessee because the mountainous terrain reminded them of the old country and because the people of this area reminded them of the people of Palestine—peasant-like and easy-going, not city slickers.

Their fresh, daily-made food became a hit with both students and locals. Renee's specialties included shish tawook, a chicken in a pita, and mujidra (sautéed lentils, rice and onions), as well as the Middle Eastern dishes of falafel, tabbouleh, shawarma sandwiches and kafta. The maza was a sampler of six appetizers, and guests could choose from items such as baba ghannouj, fattoush, spinach fatayer (spinach and cheese–stuffed pastries), stuffed grape leaves or hummus. Popular desserts at the Falafel Hut were baklawa, or baklava, as well as hareeseh, a sweet semolina cake described by locals as having the consistency of corn bread. For the not so adventurous eaters, the menu also included deli sandwiches, ham and eggs and steaks. Guests could top off their meal with a cup of rich Arabic coffee, said to be thick enough to float a spoon on.

The original location of the Falafel Hut was destroyed by fire, and the Jubrans relocated the popular eatery to 601 Fifteenth, now James Agee Street. In 2007, after twenty-five years of business, they put the Falafel House—along with their other businesses, Sam's Party Store and a laundromat—up for sale. The buildings, names, furnishings and equipment were listed at $975,000. The Falafel House reopened in 2008 with new

Hawkeye's Corner menu. *McClung Historical Collection.*

owner Mike Soueid. By 2009, the space had been taken by Chaiyo's Thai and Sushi restaurant.

At 1717 White Avenue, there was Hawkeye's Corner, run by Tom Short and Charles Ericson from 1983 to 2000. Hawkeye's Corner was named for Alan Alda's character in the popular television show *M*A*S*H*. Short related that they sat underneath a tree on the property one day and came up with the name, singling out Alda's character, which they interpreted as clever, cute, attractive and "purely wild."

Hawkeye's offered "A New Beef on Life," referring to a menu item of a roast beef sandwich. The clever menu continued with Enticelizers; Sammitches; and Delectables such as Chuck Ground to a Halt, Hickory Chickory Dock, Jive Turkey, Chick Me Out, Pita Wabbit, Shrimple Simon, Fry Me a River, Teri's Yaki Chicken, Hup 2-3-4 and a Nimwad Special. Drinks were named for characters on the show, including the B.J. Honeycutt (rum and orange and lemon juices), Major Winchester (rum, Pimm's Cup and apple juice), Colonel Potter (grapefruit juice and vodka), Radar O'Reilly (orange juice and vodka), Major Burns (Cuervo Gold tequila, "with a bite"), Hot Lips (amaretto, Bailey's Irish Cream and coffee) and Hawkeye's Special (martini in a mug). The marketing included an image of a cherry covered with a Band-Aid.

Although zaniness seemed to rule at Hawkeye's, Short was a serious restaurateur who served as president of the Greater Knoxville Restaurant Association and co-chairman of a culinary event at the Dogwood Arts Festival called Knoxville a la Carte.

While today UT's Strip is lined with a flurry of fast-food franchises, many remember the mystique of Cumberland Avenue as a place to pick up that latest record album, listen to a new band or sit and chat with friends over a great home-style meal.

CHAPTER 17

BEARDEN AND BEYOND

"Go West for Lunch!" one restaurant ad proclaimed. And go west they did. One of the first major shopping centers located out of downtown Knoxville was Western Plaza, at 4320 Kingston Pike, which was built in 1957. The addition of the mega West Town Mall, which was built at 7600 Kingston Pike and opened in 1972, sparked a retail boom for West Knoxville, drawing business significantly from the downtown area. The Bearden District became home to thirty shopping centers and 1,500,000 square feet of office space. New construction, plenty of space and free parking lured folks away from downtown.

Several restaurants operated at Western Plaza. The Rathskeller opened in the lower level in 1958. Bavarian music filled the dining room in the German-themed eatery. The chef offered a complimentary cup of cabbage and mushroom soup to guests to start. The ziltoff salad featured finely chopped greens combined with German red cabbage, topped with a buttermilk, sour cream and chive dressing and served with thinly sliced garlic toast. Other salads were Swedish cucumber; artichoke and mushroom; or romaine, egg and anchovies. A sampling of three German sausages came on the wurst platter, while the sauerbraten featured slices of marinated beef in a sour cream gravy, served with a potato pancake and sauerkraut. Wienerschnitzel was a dish of breaded and sautéed veal medallions topped with a pouched egg, anchovies and capers. The Rathskeller was also known as a great place to have a steak, as well as Bavarian chicken, lamb chops or seafood. For dessert, guests might choose

Rathskeller menu. *McClung Historical Collection.*

a crisp apple strudel, Bavarian fruitcake (a dish similar to a Boston cream pie filled with fruit) or peach schnapps ice cream.

A fire destroyed the business in 1973, but the Rathskeller reopened in 1976, going all out with its old-world décor, featuring a hand-painted mural of a crest flanked by lions, large murals of Old Heidelberg, paintings of summer and winter Bavarian scenes and Bavarian art. Archways, a soaring cathedral ceiling and turrets added to the outside of the building presented a castle look. After closing and opening one more time, the Rathskeller closed for good in 1982, following the conclusion of the World's Fair.

The Half Shell, House of Oyster and Beef, was opened in 1975 by Calvin Shipe, a recent University of Tennessee graduate, and Jess Ward, who had been in the restaurant business for fourteen years. Ward noted that he had collected recipes from California to the Bahamas for seven years in anticipation of being able to open his own place. They opened in a Tudor-style building at 5201 Homberg Drive that had formerly been an art gallery. The steak and seafood restaurant became very popular, and guests came by the droves for the excellent food and service. Two years after opening, the owners had doubled the size and seating capacity of the restaurant and encouraged reservations, stating they had no more slow nights.

Half Shell menu. *McClung Historical Collection.*

The Half Shell served platters of oysters in various styles—the creamy spinach-covered Rockefeller, the cheese-crusted Bienville and the tomato-coated Casino. Strip steak, prime rib, crab legs and lobster were also menu staples. Each dinner was accompanied by an oyster soup, salad with house-made dressing and fresh bread. Combination platters were a popular option for diners to mix and match dinner selections. Featured desserts were a lime Bavarian pie, walnut cake and Bananas Foster served flaming tableside.

Additional partners were brought into the business, including Alan Christison, a business and computer expert who designed programs necessary for the operation of the restaurant, and Brett Coffman. The group suffered a devastating loss on the morning of December 21, 1985, when a fire erupted in the building, caused by an electronic cash register that had been installed only two weeks prior. The fire burned for three hours, being difficult to extinguish because the building had been renovated many times with the extensive use of false ceilings. The ten-thousand-square-foot building was a complete loss. Being the busy holiday season, the Half Shell had reservations that day for ninety guests for lunch and four hundred for dinner.

Without even taking time to mourn the loss, the owners and employees sprang into action in hopes to save the busy week of service. The old Rathskeller building was empty, and former owner Bob Chapman had been through a fire and knew exactly what the group was going through. He handed the keys to Shipe and told him to "do what you want with it." Employees brought in supplies and mopped, swept and cleaned to get the new space ready. Inspections were done, the liquor license was transferred, menus were printed and a special shipment of food was brought in from Nashville. City officials assisted the business in moving quickly.

The Half Shell operated out of the temporary space for a while and then opened in a location farther west at Fort Loudoun. Meanwhile, they began construction on a new building in Western Plaza. It was to be a large restaurant, able to seat 350 guests. The design for the new building was in the shape of an oyster shell. The floor plan fanned out from the center bar area. There was an upstairs and several fireplaces.

Business was good at the marina location, with seven to eight hundred guests on a Friday night, and some employees opted to stay there while some came back to work in Bearden. Tragedy struck when co-owner Alan Christison was on his way to the Fort Loudoun location and his car was struck by a train. He died from the injuries on February 14, 1986.

The loss of his friend and business partner was very difficult for Shipe. He related that all they had been through was enough to make a person turn bitter. A plaque was created in honor of Christison and hung in the foyer of the new Half Shell restaurant. It stated that the building was dedicated to the memory of Alan Christison, who had helped in planning it. After success, turmoil and tragedy, the Half Shell closed in 1991.

By 1992, a new concept was being brought into the former Half Shell space. Kiva Grill was developed by Jim Huff, who had a hand in many businesses in Gatlinburg, such as the Applewood Farmhouse Restaurant, the Burning Bush, Brass Lantern, LeConte Lodge and Mountain View Hotel. Kiva was a Native American word for a ceremonial hut or hall of feasts and celebrations, with a high center or ceiling. The Kiva Grill was to be a play on the popular Southwest style of the time in décor as well as cuisine. Huff had been planning the concept for several years and made trips to Santa Fe to study the food and culture of the area.

The new look of the space included stucco walls, adobe colors, Navajo rugs, earthenware pottery and folk art. A fashion show of Southwest clothing and entertainment by a classical guitarist were featured during the grand opening, but food was the real star of the show at Kiva Grill. Emphasis was on grilled fish and meats, spices and various peppers, as well as fresh vegetables.

Black bean soup, of all things, was the rage in restaurants in the early '90s. Kiva Grill featured a Desert Painted black bean soup, topped with adoba red chile sauce and crème fraiche and served with a traditional Indian flatbread and a creamy spread. Other menu items included blue corn lobster cakes with black bean salsa, duck and goat cheese quesadillas, calamari battered with blue cornmeal, shrimp diablo, chicken mole, grilled pork loin with barbacoa (barbecue) sauce, lamb chops with tomatillo chutney and roasted quail. Entrées were accompanied by patty pan squash and either roasted herb potatoes or green chile mashed potatoes. Desserts included frozen lime soufflé, caramel flan, margarita cheesecake and homemade ice cream.

This Southwest style was associated with many Knoxville restaurants in the '90s, so much so that many almost considered it the Knoxville style. Chefs did it well, and East Tennesseans loved the flavors. Tim Love was brought in as the new chef at Kiva Grill, but only shortly before it closed. His Southwest style would have to wait a bit to shine.

In 1998, the building at Western Plaza became the home of the Blackhorse Pub, owned by Jeff and Sherri Robinson, who had opened their first location in Clarksville in 1992. The name stems from the Eleventh Armored Cavalry Regiment, the Blackhorse Regiment. By 2002, the Blackhorse had gone back to operating only out of the Clarksville location. The Green Hills Grille, One Tree Grille and Sequoyah Grille all tried out the space before the Blackhorse returned, fifteen years later, in 2013. Robinson related that a friend sent him the news story of Sequoyah Grille closing with a note saying it was a chance for Robinson to "fix your mistake" and return to Knoxville.

Elsewhere in Bearden, brothers Shawqi and Ruad Bahou from Jerusalem opened their Bahou Restaurant on Forest Avenue in 1971, followed by the Bahou Container, a gourmet café featuring carryout items, at 5128 Homberg Drive in 1973. With their restaurants, the Bahous were ushering new food experiences into the city. One review noted, "Eggplant and artichoke don't taste as bad as they sound." Eggplant and artichoke, along with Bahou's Cauliflower Arabesque (fried cauliflower soaked in tahini and lemon), would fit right in with our modern food trends of today. In 1975, the brothers opened a restaurant at Lennox Square and South Lake Mall in Atlanta. Recipes of dishes served there—Apricot Pudding and Bathejan II (eggplant and crabmeat casserole)—were requested by readers and printed in *Gourmet* magazine.

In 1978, the new Bahou's Mediterranean Restaurant opened at 5200 Kingston Pike. Design features of the eatery were four porcelain over steel columns, patterned from a Persian rug and hand stenciled. The ceiling over the bar was stamped steel from a hundred-year-old pattern by a Brooklyn company. In 1983, Shawqi and Ruad remodeled it to an ice cream shop called Scoops before selling all their restaurants that same year and each taking a different path. The building has since been home to many dining establishments—McGillicuddy's, Rhapsody's, Tuscany, Bistro by the Tracks, Chez Liberty and Shuck Raw Bar.

Richard Lakin opened Richard's in Homberg in 1985. So you thought wild game being served in a restaurant in Knoxville was a new thing? Not so. Richard's offered what the *East Tennessee Business Journal* called a "strange menu," including entrées of Australian boar, alligator, bear paw stew, beaver, elk, peacock, rattlesnake, reindeer, Scotch woodcock, dormice, Ohio River muskrat and even an African lion dinner for $22.95. I'll stop there. The huge menu contained sixty-three different entrées and could take guests up to twenty minutes to read through. All the employees of Richard's had previously worked in hotels where they were tired of creativity being stifled, noting that there were even memos on how thin to slice the tomatoes. More conventional diners might have chosen a dish called Breast of Venus— chicken breast sautéed with maple syrup and ginger topped with two sunny side up quail eggs.

Farther west, and considered the outskirts of West Knoxville at the time, at 8361 Kingston Pike, a Middle Eastern deli was opened by brothers Nazeeh and Nabih Aqqad. Before coming to Tennessee, Nazeeh ran a 350-seat restaurant in Kuwait. While there, he gained culinary influence from chefs from France, Lebanon, Syria and Jerusalem. When Nazeeh left Kuwait, he was unable to return to his homeland of war-torn Jerusalem. The brothers opened Ali Baba Time Out Delicatessen one week after Nazeeh arrived in Knoxville. The Aqqads liked their new life in America, Nazeeh stating that he enjoyed the freedom here and that he didn't like fighting.

Nabih had come to the United States in 1971. He could not speak English at the time and went to the International House at the University of Tennessee for six months to learn. He later became an American citizen. Nabih's business philosophy was to offer something different. He also did not spend money on television or newspaper advertising, preferring to put extra money back into the food by giving customers a little more meat or lettuce or tomato. Nabih had figured out that word of mouth was so important in advertising, especially in Knoxville, stating, "Word gets around. That way it pays off ten times over." It was also important to the brothers to handle all the business operations themselves, noting that it was hard to find cooks to create their Middle Eastern dishes and that some employees didn't care if customers came back or not, and they wanted customers coming back.

The brothers took the name of their eatery from the story of Ali Baba and the Forty Thieves, from the collection of fairy tales *1001 Arabian Nights*. Nabih's dream was to eventually have a restaurant where the door could not be opened as usual but patrons would have to—just as in the story to get into the thieves' den—use the phrase "Open Sesame" to be admitted. When guests entered, the inside would look like a dream, like something from a fairy tale. In forty successful years of business, not much changed at Ali Baba's except a remodel of the floor. The Aqqads closed Ali Baba's in 2013. The building was torn down to be replaced with two buildings housing national retail chains.

At 9000 Kingston Pike, in the Cedar Bluff area, the historic Baker-Peters-Rogers House was developed into a restaurant in 1977. The house was built in 1840 for Dr. and Mrs. Harvey Baker and then later passed on to the George Peters family, then the V.M. Rogers family. First of all, is it haunted? By most accounts, the answer would be yes. Did that stop anyone from doing business there? That answer would be definitely not.

The presence of paranormal activity is usually reported by the general public in places where trauma or great tragedy occurred. During the Civil War, Dr. Baker's son Abner fought for the South, and Dr. Baker also treated wounded Confederates. When Union soldiers arrived at Dr. Baker's home, he tried in vain to convince them that he was a private citizen, merely doing his job. The Union soldiers shot and killed Dr. Baker in an upstairs bedroom of the house. When Abner returned home after the war, he tracked down one of the local soldiers, who had become a postmaster in Knoxville, and shot him. The remaining former soldiers ambushed Abner. Reports were that they tied him to a team of horses and dragged him until he was dead; others reported Abner died by hanging. Either one of those endings provides a traumatic story.

Another century and world away, in 1977, Jack Slagle built a modern realty office building across the street from the old antebellum home. He often admired the home, its history and mystery, and when he heard someone was planning to buy the house and tear it down, he took immediate action and purchased the home himself. Slagle and Gary Trusler developed the first restaurant in the home, called Jeremiah's, featuring seven dining rooms. After suffering a heart attack, Slagle sold Jeremiah's in 1979 to the owners of the Half Shell, who changed the menu from steak and seafood to specializing in New Orleans–style

Left: Jeremiah's menu. *McClung Historical Collection.*

Below: Jeremiah's ad. *McClung Historical Collection.*

barbecue. By 1982, the space had evolved again as the second location of Hawkeye's Corner.

In 1989, the property was purchased by Phillips Petroleum, which had plans to demolish the home and build a gas station, convenience store and car wash. After public outcry arose, a Farragut alderman put forth a proposal to have the Baker-Peters House moved six miles west for use as a library and town museum for Farragut in order to save the building and protect it in perpetuity. In the end, a plan was worked out with Phillips to save the home and still have room for its facilities. Rex Bradford Jones opened Abner's Attic in the house in 1990.

Jones was an experienced restaurateur who created an experience for his guests. In the historic setting, servers were outfitted in period dress. The walls of the dining rooms were teal with large floral wall borders. The cloth tablecloths were matched to the fabric in the drapery swags. Individual terry cloth hand towels were available in the ladies' room. Portions of Jones's signature dish, the Southern Puff—grits with herbs rolled into a ball and fried in a way similar to hushpuppies—were served at the beginning of every meal.

Abner's Attic was a heart-healthy restaurant in conjunction with St. Mary's Medical Center. The menu specifically noted tips for healthier eating and marked menu items that were in accordance with the heart-healthy program. The popular Plantation Delight was half a pineapple filled with fresh fruit and cottage cheese. Lean ground turkey burgers and grilled chicken kept with the heart-healthy program, while the 1860 Layered Salad of fresh lettuce, green peas, celery, onions, green pepper, American and Swiss cheese, bacon and mayonnaise kept with the historic southern theme.

At the time that Hawkeye's and Abner's Attic occupied the Baker-Peters House, there were many reported instances of unexplained phenomena. Doors would open and close and lights and calculators would go off and on by themselves, books and glasses would fly off the shelves several feet away, items would be found moved to different places and people reported hearing footsteps, whistling, screams and even laughter. Some even reported seeing a man dressed in a gray cloak inside the building. As Jones began to acknowledge and pay small tributes to Abner, hanging a picture of him and naming menu items for him, the unexplained activity lessened.

By 1993, Jones had closed Abner's Attic but eventually relocated it to another home on the Asheville Highway in 2007. Krystyna's, an Eastern- and Central European–influenced restaurant; the Painted Table by Don and Lauren DeVore and Steve Mynatt; and the Baker Peters Jazz Club

Michael's Cow Palace, West Knoxville. *McClung Historical Collection.*

were other occupants of the Baker-Peters House, continuing its tradition as an eatery.

An article from 1988 stated that some people said downtown was dying, but it wasn't from starvation. Its accompanying map displayed fifty-one downtown eateries; however, they were mostly lunch spots for downtown workers. Restaurants of all other cuisines and concepts continued opening around Bearden, the Cedar Bluff area and farther west.

CHAPTER 18

DINNER AND A SHOW

The dinner theater concept came into being in Knoxville in the 1960s, with the idea of pairing good food with professionally produced versions of popular Broadway plays. The Barn Theater was the first dinner theater to be built in Knoxville in 1966. It was a $100,000 structure on Kingston Pike near Dixie Lee Junction and was described as a big red barn with a farm wagon parked in the front—probably similar to every other field in the then very rural west part of Knoxville.

Barn Theaters was a dinner theater franchise begun by Howard D. Wolfe, who had been a student at the University of Tennessee in the 1940s. He already had locations in twelve states, including Georgia, North Carolina and Virginia. Mr. and Mrs. Charles Rhea were the owners of the new franchise. Both the show and the menu were to change every four weeks.

Sir Jack Squires was the executive chef at the Barn. The play *Never Too Late* opened the theater, accompanied by rock Cornish hen, roast beef, Malayan curried fruit, parsley potatoes, asparagus with drawn butter, Caesar salad, macaroni and shrimp salad, breads, rolls, dessert and coffee. The box office opened at 6:30 p.m., the dinner buffet began at 7:00 p.m. and the performance began at 8:30 p.m. Seating was available for 288 guests. A later menu featured shrimp Louie, curried chicken à la Florentine and strawberry seafoam salad.

Dinner seating was at tables on elevated risers surrounding an opening in the center where the buffet was set up. The buffet was broken down and cleared after dinner, and the set for the show, with actors already intact, was lowered down from the barn loft by pulleys.

WEST SIDE
DINNER THEATRE

BUFFET DINNER 6:30 - 8:00
CURTAIN 8:30

HELLO,
DOLLY!

performances nightly
tuesday - saturday

FOR RESERVATIONS
PHONE 966-6731

12801 KINGSTON PIKE

West Side Dinner Theatre. *McClung Historical Collection.*

At the same location, 12801 Kingston Pike, the West Side Dinner Theater opened in 1976 to a sold-out show of *Fiddler on the Roof.* The theater was under the direction of Don Gwyn. A buffet dinner ran from 6:45 to 8:00 p.m., with a play starting at 8:30 p.m. Admission included both the dinner and show ticket. Prices began at ten dollars for Tuesday through Thursday and twelve dollars for Friday and Saturday.

The buffet at the West Side Dinner included three entrées, four vegetables, five or six salads and a couple of desserts. The House Specialty was Steamboat Round of Roast Beef that was served with, among others, sweet and sour pork, baked Icelandic cod, oven baked potatoes, broccoli spears with cheese, spiced apples, corn pudding, bean salad and assorted salad fixings, relish tray, cheesecake and banana pudding.

Seating for 275 was available in the theater, which was "in the round," as tables were placed in tiers surrounding the stage in the center of the room. It sounds odd by today's standards, but the second Thursday of each show was designated Non-Smokers' Night. Productions included *The Owl and the Pussycat, The Odd Couple, Bus Stop, The Sunshine Boys, The Sound of Music, A Funny Thing Happened on the Way to the Forum* and *Cat on a Hot Tin Roof.*

In 1982, the theater moved to Papermill Drive after losing its lease at the Kingston Pike location. The building was remodeled for $80,000 to be in the dinner theater style, featuring a retractable stage. The audience sat three-quarters of the way around it. The buffet was set up on roller tables so that after dinner was over, the tables could be rolled away and the stage rolled out.

The new theater space got off to a great start with a tour group of one hundred guests booked for opening night. Being the year of Knoxville's World's Fair, forty to fifty other tour groups coming in for the fair were in discussion about attending shows at the theater. But by 1983, attendance had begun to wane, and the once popular attraction closed temporarily and then operated off and on through the '80s and '90s.

In 1980, there was talk of putting a dinner theater in the old Riviera Theater at 510 Gay Street. The building had been constructed in 1886 and remodeled into a one-thousand-seat movie theater in 1920. The movie theater had closed in 1976, and it was torn down in 1988. The grand revival of the Riviera Theater was yet to come.

The Terrace Dinner Theater was opened in 1980 by Jim Simpson at 315 Mohican in Homberg Place. The space was the former Capri Terrace movie theater, which was built in 1973. The property took its name from the extensive terracing in the landscaping. Tiered seating in the round was available for three hundred guests, and the venture featured a Tuesday-through-Saturday buffet at 6:00 p.m., with the show starting at 8:30 p.m. Sunday brunch began at noon, with a show starting at 2:00 p.m. A lounge with a bar was created out of the theater lobby, where patrons formerly purchased popcorn, candy and soft drinks.

As far as food was concerned, the Terrace went all out, hiring former Cherokee Country Club chef Terry Kuester. Kuester had first come to the Knoxville area to be the general manager of a restaurant in the McGhee Tyson Airport called Sky Chefs. He had previously been part of the Hilton Hotel management training program. Kuester trained at the Palmer House in Chicago and in 1961 was chosen to oversee the preparation of a meal for President John F. Kennedy. During his ten years at the Cherokee Country Club, he estimated serving over one million meals to members and guests.

Kuester's inaugural buffet at the Terrace featured chef-carved roast beef, Louisiana shrimp Creole with saffron rice and coq au vin accompanied by an assortment of vegetables, a salad bar and homemade blueberry muffins, rolls and corn bread. The Sunday brunch offerings included baked and sliced ham, sausage, bacon, chicken casserole, scrambled eggs, biscuits and their accompaniments.

The opening show at the Terrace was the *Can Can*, followed by *Life with Father*, *Sleuth*, *A Gershwin Revue*, *Blithe Spirit*, *Play It Again Sam* and *Kiss Me Kate*. After a one-year run, Simpson changed the format from producing live theater performances to showing second-run movies.

Simpson also changed the name of the theater to Terrace Draft House Theater but in 1982 was forced to change the name again due to a legal dispute. An attorney from Atlanta representing Cinema 'n Draft House noted that the name, for public identity purposes, was identical to his client's business name. Simpson changed the name to Terrace Tap House Theater. The Terrace Tap House was eventually reportedly smelling of stale beer and cigarettes and showing scratched second-run movies flanked by faded curtains. The Terrace Tap House had to go, and it was replaced by simply the Terrace Theater.

Eventually, in 1999, a new concept, the Cinema Grill franchise, was brought to Knoxville to fill the space. The idea was to continue showing second-run movies, but instead of the usual theater-type seating, to have guests seated at counters or tables with swivel chairs and served food in the style of T.G.I. Fridays or Applebees, such as burgers, sandwiches and pizzas. It closed within the year.

PART VII

New Dining Trends and a Touch of Class

CHAPTER 19

KRISTOPHER KENDRICK'S CONTINENTAL STYLE

$\mathcal{D}$oes Knoxville have scruples? Well, we once had a restaurant named Scruples. It was part of the new dining trend of Knoxville restaurants serving continental cuisine. Piccolo's at the Pembroke, the Volador and other continental-type restaurants began to emerge around town in the 1970s and '80s.

Knoxville's absolute king of continental style was Kristopher Kendrick. In 1971, he opened his landmark restaurant, the Orangery, at 5412 Kingston Pike. It was the first business partnership of Kendrick and a precocious twenty-two-year-old budding chef, Frank Gardner of Rogersville.

Kristopher Kendrick has been called the godfather of Knoxville preservation. Born in Oak Ridge, everything in the "Secret City" was new construction during World War II, which created in Kendrick a fascination for everything old. Some of his restoration projects include the Bistro at the Bijou, the Peter Kern Building/St. Oliver Hotel, Patrick Sullivan's, the Emporium, the Medical Arts Building, the Dulin home/Dulin Art Gallery, the Nicholas, Kendrick Place, King's Row, the River House, the Cunningham, the Stuart, Park Place, the Lucerne, the A. Percy Lockett home (Lord Lindsey) and the Old City Club. His daughter Karen said that her father saw beauty in a lot of things that others did not see the beauty in. As for the Orangery, Karen noted, "He wanted it to be a place where everybody was gracious and kind, not pretentious or stuffy."

For years, I was a member of a ladies' luncheon group that met every month at the Orangery, along with every other ladies' luncheon group

Above: Volador menu. *McClung Historical Collection.*

Left: The Orangery ad. *McClung Historical Collection.*

in town, which was exactly the clientele for which Kendrick created the Orangery—the ladies who lunch. Kendrick already owned a successful hair salon and clothing boutique, but some of his patrons had expressed a desire for a nice comfortable place to relax after shopping. The ultimate decisive moment came when Kendrick saw three of his clients entering an inelegant dining establishment for lunch. He decided then and there to create a chic, elegant dining room.

The name for the restaurant was taken from a book Kendrick found in his collection that noted that Marie Antoinette called a small chateau at Versailles where she kept her orange trees in the winter the Orangery. The building itself began as an old Quonset hut, built for the John Deere Tractor Company during World War II. Kendrick bought the structure in 1966 and began transforming it over time to a beautiful, Palladian-style building. He outfitted the dining room with his own personal collection of antiques from his travels around the world and local architectural treasures he acquired from demolition sites of old mansions, saving everything old and beautiful that he could.

Kendrick and Gardner took a simplistic approach to beginning their restaurant. They bought a four-burner stove from a scratch and dent sale, an oven and an old antique worktable to outfit the ten- by fifteen-foot kitchen. Gardner noted that he had a repertoire of about seven good recipes at the time. They went to the A&P, bought groceries and opened.

Gardner first learned about cooking from his uncle William Gardner, who was a gourmet cook in San Francisco. He also studied with Gloria Wright DuBoyce, the niece of architect Frank Lloyd Wright, while he was working as a groundskeeper at her estate in St. Thomas, Virgin Islands. Additionally, Gardner used his spare time to study cookbooks, sometimes up to two hours a day. He later made several trips abroad to study in France. When the Orangery first opened, Gardner would ask guests what they would like to see served there, and then, consulting Julia Child's *Mastering the Art of French Cooking* and other classic French cookbooks, he would learn to make it and call them up to tell them it was now on the menu. Intentionally catering to its guests, the Orangery was an instant hit.

There was no more written about or reviewed restaurant in Knoxville than the Orangery. From the lavish and ornate décor and classical music played in the background to table arrangements of fresh cut flowers and real sugar bowls filled with granulated sugar, the Orangery made an impression. By 1975, the acclaimed eatery had been named by *Gentlemen's Quarterly* magazine as one of the top twenty-five restaurants in the United States and one of the top thirty-two in the world.

The Orangery assembled a collection of seven chefs who worked under Gardner's philosophy that "cooking is a creative art rather than a technical skill." Because of limited space and refrigeration in the tiny kitchen, Gardner would visit the market twice a day to purchase fresh vegetables. Veal, pheasant and quail were obtained from local growers.

Gigot d'agneau or succulent slices of leg of lamb; Cornish hen with sausage dressing and a sweet chestnut purée; Coquilles St. Jacques, or large scallops flamed in a cognac and mushroom cream sauce; Oyster-Artichoke Ramekin topped with a special sauce made of oyster liquor, cream and sherry and topped with parmesan cheese and almonds; and even sweetbreads made appearances on the menu. A dinner favorite was chicken supremes de Volaille—boned chicken breasts sautéed quickly in butter and then covered with a rich, white and velvety veloute sauce. Sides were, among others, asparagus parmesan, creamed spinach or sliced fresh carrots cooked in chicken broth and seasoned with brown sugar and nutmeg. Gardner was sometimes known to use three gallons of whipping cream a night in his desserts.

With the success of the Orangery, Kendrick's daughter Karen took over the day-to-day operations while Kristopher went on to develop another restaurant in 1976, Lord Lindsey, at 615 West Hill Avenue. The large, tall, white-columned building was the former home of A. Percy Lockett, which he had built in 1903 as a wedding gift for his fiancée, in the style of her childhood antebellum home in Mississippi. The Locketts eventually moved farther downriver to a larger residence, the Armstrong-Lockett House, now Crescent Bend, and the home was converted into the First Church of Christ Scientist in 1929. With his restoration of the building, Kendrick received the first Knoxville Adaptation Award.

Charles Lord Lindsey was the official name of Kendrick's new establishment, and I wish I could have seen it in its glory. A black-and-white diamond-patterned floor with oyster-white walls and stark white woodwork made up the dining room. Furnishings and appointments were from old New York hotels, such as china place settings and sterling silver from the St. Regis and Chippendale chairs and Louis XV bombe chests from the River Club. A large crystal chandelier and oriental rugs contributed to the elegant theme.

The Lord Lindsey was known for fine dining, dancing, special events and catering and in the '90s even offered Valentine's Day Breakfast in

Bed. Chocolate-covered strawberries, croissants, muffins and Danish accompanied by fresh orange juice and a rose would be delivered by a tuxedoed waiter who would serve the fare and then leave discreetly.

The Lord Lindsey catering operation eventually moved out of the old home and later closed. The historic building was bought by developer Tony Cappiello in 2010 and later put up for sale.

Gardner was on to other projects as well. In 1977, he opened Hanna's restaurant in the old Ross Hanna mansion at 120 Ebenezer Road. This property had the merit of being the childhood home of animal expert Jack Hanna, who became the well-known director of the Columbus Zoo and made regular television appearances with Johnny Carson and David Letterman. Guests would pass horses and ponies in the fields along the long, winding driveway leading into Hanna's, and at the entrance was a tree where four beautiful macaws resided. They were later replaced with doves.

Some called Hanna's the classiest restaurant ever opened in Knoxville but also noted that it seemed too classy for Knoxvillians, which would play into its demise. Gardner later went on to open the Union Café at the

The Union Café ad. *McClung Historical Collection.*

Arnstein Building next to Market Square in 1980 with Chicago restaurateur Jim Smith. Called by Gardner American and Continental, it was noted as the first restaurant of its kind in downtown Knoxville. He then went on to operate restaurants in Gatlinburg before returning to partner again with Kendrick to open Patrick Sullivan's in the Old City. Gardner became a big proponent of the Old City through the '90s and also owned Manhattan's and Lucille's. His last Old City restaurant, El Camino, in the Southwest style, closed in 2002.

The Orangery was going strong in the '80s and in 1984 won a prestigious Four Star Award from *Mobil Travel Guide*, being the only Knoxville restaurant to receive such an honor. The following year, however, a fire set by an arsonist ravaged the Orangery. Most of Kristopher Kendrick's priceless antiques and treasures, collected over a quarter of a century, were lost. Over one hundred Louis XVI chairs from the ballroom of the Grand Hotel in Paris, English sofas and chairs, Italian sculptures and furniture, paintings, tapestries, oriental rugs, French armoires and mirrors, marble-topped tables and a twenty-five- by twelve-foot wall taken from an Argentine palace that once belonged to Eva and Juan Peron topped with fringe and tassels from the Palm Beach home of Isabel Dodge Sloan of the automotive family—all gone, in addition to all of his business records.

Kendrick was in shock that anyone could do such a thing as purposely set the destructive, devastating fire but planned to rebuild right away. A longtime friend and former employee related that the fire had "broken his heart."

While the Orangery was being rebuilt, dinner service was conducted out of another of Kendrick's establishments, the Old City Club, at 612 South Gay Street. Kendrick had opened the private club in 1984 for downtown professionals and business people as a space for breakfast meetings and power lunches. The Old City Club closed in 1992 after Kendrick realized he had spent at least a quarter of a million dollars on it with not enough return.

Within seventeen months, Kendrick had rebuilt the Orangery, again in the Palladian style, at the cost of $2.5 million. A few items survived the fire and were incorporated in the new building: the Chinese red front doors from London's Eaton Square, a spiral staircase from a pre–Civil War home, large Palladian windows from the old Park Bank and brick flooring from a turn-of-the-century horse auction house. The new building had even more architectural grandeur and complexity than the original. The ceiling was painted in three shades of blue to give a sky effect. Tennessee pink marble from the Craig quarry was used for bar and table tops, sending a nod back to Knoxville's legacy as a leader in the marble industry of the late 1800s

Kiger's ad/menu. *McClung Historical Collection.*

and early 1900s. Etched in a pink marble plaque beside the entrance were the words "Conceptions. Visions. Dreams.," which completely captured the essence of Kendrick.

By 2009, Karen Kendrick, newly married and with her aging father in poor health, was looking to sell the Orangery. It was bought by local businessman David Kiger, who was a boat dealer and owner of three marinas. Kiger had previously owned another restaurant, Kiger's at Willow Point Marina.

The best-selling dish at the Orangery when it opened in 1971 was the Hot Shrimp Salad Sandwich, which is, coincidentally, the last meal I had there before it unexpectedly closed for good in 2016. The dish had been created by Frank Gardner forty-five years earlier and was an open-faced sandwich of shrimp, olives, French mayonnaise and chives, topped with Gruyere cheese and melted in the oven. Women reportedly came to the restaurant five days a week for that particular sandwich.

Kristopher Kendrick passed away in 2009 at age seventy-four. He once stated, "I basically do things based on emotion. I never know why I do a lot of the things I do." We are extremely grateful for the work of Kristopher Kendrick and his dedication to the preservation of the historic beauty of Knoxville. Take a walk around town, and on nearly every street, you'll find a bit of Kristopher Kendrick's style.

CHAPTER 20

THE ENVIRONMENT

THE ULTIMATE OUTDOOR PATIO

African lions aren't for eating, silly; they're for admiring while noshing on an avocado stuffed with fresh fruit, alfalfa sprouts and a light dressing. I was standing in line in a shop when the man next to me immediately recognized the decades-old menus I was holding marked "The Environment" and called out, "Oh, that was at the zoo!" The Knoxville Zoo once had a reputation for its inventive and well-designed restaurant with a beautiful view in lush surroundings accompanied by fresh and flavorful high-quality food. In fact, opening day of the Environment Restaurant consisted of Lobster Newburg on the menu and rare Siberian tigers on the vista.

The Environment was the brainchild of the then zoo director, Guy Smith, and his wife, Patty, to create one of the first sit-down restaurants in a zoo, with both indoor and outdoor patio eating areas. The building for the eatery was constructed entirely by zoo personnel in 1977. It had a sloping roof, to keep with the theme of the zoo, and a rustic, timbered look in order to blend in with the wooded surroundings.

An air-conditioned indoor dining room could seat around fifty guests and featured large floor-to-ceiling windows that overlooked the zoo exhibits. An expansive outdoor eating deck could seat another seventy-some guests. The area was filled with flora such as trees coming up through the deck, dogwoods and redbuds, along with caladiums, azaleas and new plantings of tulips contributing to the beauty of the area.

The Environment was one of the first restaurants in Knoxville to have patio dining. And this wasn't just any patio. Guests were able to enjoy dining while overlooking the African Plains exhibit of five African elephants, four zebras and four eland or large antelope. Tigers, emu and an aviary exhibit were also on view at this one-of-a-kind eatery.

Guests dining at the Environment did not have to pay admission to the zoo in order to eat at the restaurant and did not have to walk through the zoo to get to the restaurant. Patrons were directed to enter on Castle Street, off Magnolia Avenue, to a special parking area easily accessible to the eatery.

Ingrid Arnett was the first manager of the Environment. She arranged interesting lunch items for guests, including a Safari Sandwich, which was a combination of three meats plus cheeses and assorted salad items; Quiche Lorraine; and even Knoxville's signature Metts and Beans, but dinner was the real star. After 5:00 p.m., items such as water chestnuts wrapped in chicken liver and bacon, creamed herring, escargot, a seven- or nine-ounce filet mignon, a four- or twelve-ounce ribeye, golden roasted rock Cornish hen, trout almandine, succulent lobster tail and quiche aux fruits der mer (seafood quiche with lobster, shrimp and white fish, a recipe from the South of France) were served.

Rex Bradford Jones took over operations of the Environment in 1978. He brought in his mother, Frances Wylie Jones, who had been the home service director for the Knoxville Utility Board (KUB), to help out. She did such a good job with quality control that he convinced her to stay on as manager. In her services for the KUB, Jones had helped with introducing electric appliances and lights into the community and had a mobile kitchen she took about for instructional purposes. I have discovered many surprises while researching Knoxville, but when I asked Rex what his mother was teaching folks with the mobile kitchen, he responded with an answer that was so completely unexpected to me that I stopped writing and looked up in silence for a few seconds. When electricity was first introduced in the area through the TVA, people were afraid to cook with it. Jones helped homemakers learn how to cook with electricity.

Some of the items that Jones made specialties on the menu were the Omelette Zoopreme with guests' choice of filling; the Polynesian Delight, half a pineapple filled with melon and fresh fruit and topped with homemade chicken salad or shrimp salad; the Gourmet Delight sandwich, with bacon, avocado, tomato, onion and alfalfa sprouts on rye bread with a special dressing; or the Sprout Salad. He had a hard time acquiring sprouts in Knoxville at the time and finally found an herb farm in nearby Kodak that was growing them. Homemade soups or a stuffed croissant could be had, along with heartier items such as a pork barbecue sandwich, spaghetti, baked potatoes or burgers. Desserts were Black Forest cherry torte cake, carrot cake or walnut layer cake, among others.

Jones had the privilege of learning everything about the hospitality business from his mother. Not only was she an excellent cook who could "make divinity on a rainy day," but she also taught Rex how to develop recipes and the importance of service, place settings and presentation.

Mrs. Jones created their signature amuse, the Southern Puff—grits formed into a ball and deep fried—from leftovers from a special brunch she served to the Australian delegation to the World's Fair. She even designed skirts for the servers at the Environment made out of animal print fabrics. Mrs. Jones urged servers to be extra pleasant to guests in order to send them away with happy memories of the zoo and the city. The guest book was filled with signatures from visitors from all around the world, along with compliments on the delicious food, some noting it was "the best I've had on the trip."

Along with tourists, many locals frequented the Environment, coming from their work at downtown businesses or for chamber events, special functions, ladies' luncheons or even weddings.

The Environment closed in 1989 as business and people moved to other areas of town. Jones moved on to open Abner's Attic and then later developed a very successful catering business. His son, Bradford William Jones, joined him in Bradford Catered Events, along with ten to twelve full-time employees and seventy-five part-time employees. In 2016, they bought the Lunchbox Market & Cafe, which had been in business for thirty-five years and was being closed by the owner, Karen Sproles. Bradford wanted to incorporate the Lunch Box into their company for the thriving business it was doing, while Rex viewed it more as a continuation of an important historic business.

Just as he enjoyed working with his mother years ago, Rex gets pleasure from now working with his son, who has "brought new eyes and young blood into the business." For Rex Bradford Jones, it has always been about family, great food and experiences that create lasting memories.

CHAPTER 21

WATERFRONT FARE

*Y*ou mean that well-known eatery that has enjoyed thirty years of success along the Tennessee River wasn't the first Knoxville restaurant at 400 Neyland Drive? No, not even the second or third. The building that now houses the ever-popular Calhoun's on the River was constructed in 1981 for a restaurant called Cajun's Wharf.

The ill-fated eatery was plagued with problems from its beginning. Parking spaces were created over an area designated for use as a playground and picnic spot in the adjoining Bicentennial Park. Cars were towed from the parking lot near the restaurant. After a forty-foot heating duct fell and injured guests, the restaurant owners were ordered to replace substandard wiring. The Cajun-themed style and food of the restaurant did not represent East Tennessee, and additionally, the restroom doors were labeled "Shecrabs" and "Hecrabs."

By 1983, Cajun's Wharf was out and Buster Muggs was in. Although an ad revealed that no one had actually ever met Buster Muggs, the menu was done in the style of a newspaper, titled *The Life and Times of Buster Muggs*. The food garnered good reviews; however, a couple years later, the news was that Buster Muggs was out and *Real Seafood* was in.

Lobsters, swordfish or even the Spanish paella could not keep Real Seafood going. By 1987, it was up for sale in a foreclosure auction. Restaurateur Mike Chase realized he could buy the equipment and a long-term lease on the building for $400,000, which would have otherwise cost a couple million dollars to build, and snapped it up right away. He opened

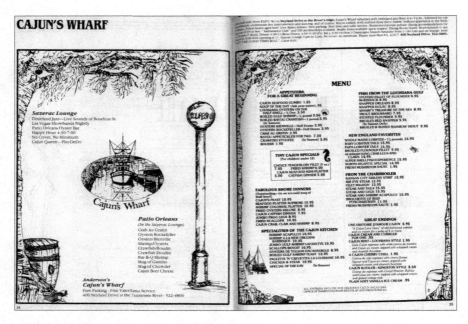

Cajun's Wharf menu. *McClung Historical Collection.*

Calhoun's on the River, which specialized in "A Taste of Tennessee," with Tennessee barbecue, ribs and steak headlining the menu.

Did you ever wonder why there is a huge lighthouse on Baum Drive? It was built as part of a restaurant. Does a pond need a lighthouse, you might ask? Not important. In 1977, Shoney's South Inc., Memphis, thought Knoxvillians needed a large, family-style seafood restaurant on the west side of town. The result was the Hungry Fisherman, at 6800 Baum Drive.

The eleven-thousand-square-foot restaurant had seating for seven hundred guests, all-you-could-eat meals and a salad bar in a boat. Guests entered through the lighthouse. There was also an outdoor playground for children featuring a merry-go-round and swing set of sea creatures, and paddle boats could be rented for seventy-five cents for a half hour. The specialty was Calabash, the breaded and deep-fried goodness folks were familiar with from the East Coast. The Hungry Fisherman developed a following through its fishing rodeos for kids and fishing tournaments with cash prizes for adults. The restaurant continued on through the '80s and then was later turned into an event center.

In the late 1980s, there began to be a call for more waterfront development along the river. Volunteer Landing was created in the 1990s, consisting of

Cajun's Wharf site on Tennessee River *(front)* and City County Building *(back)*. *Brian Stansberry.*

condominiums, a marina, boat slips, a pedestrian walkway, landscape features and the Gateway Pavilion and Regional Visitor Center, which opened in 1999. Also included in the waterfront development was a boathouse at 900 Neyland Drive, which was to be the home of the University of Tennessee women's rowing team, along with a new restaurant, the Tennessee Grill, right across from the University of Tennessee.

The restaurant was run by Emendorfer and Marks Inc., which also had the Baker-Peters Jazz Club, along with the Italian Market and Grill at Franklin Square. Bill Emendorfer had been an offensive guard and teammate of later UT football coach Phillip Fulmer for the University of Tennessee's football team from 1970 to 1972, when they won the Sugar Bowl, Liberty Bowl and Bluebonnet Bowl. He left his career as a dentist to enter the restaurant industry by opening Shoney's franchises. Barry Marks had been part of the original team that started Grady's. The cuisine was comfort food "with a regional flow."

The food at the Tennessee Grill was very appealing, featuring dishes such as hot, fresh, homemade potato chips covered with Maytag blue cheese; grilled salmon topped with a tomato basil sauce; sautéed swordfish with a delicate lemon sauce; prime rib; skewered shrimp and tenderloin; marinated sirloin; and salads of nice mixed greens filled with bacon, egg, cheese and flash-fried black-eyed peas.

The building sat right between the river and busy Neyland Drive, so on-site parking was not available. There was a plan to use valet parking or even a shuttle to transport guests to and from the restaurant, or alternately, folks could walk across using a tunnel under Neyland. I don't ever recall going through a tunnel; my friends and I would park at a lot across the street and walk over using the crosswalk. Although the Tennessee Grill was a very nice restaurant with great reviews, in the view of the general public, perhaps the parking situation couldn't quite be overcome.

Another effort was made at the space in 2007 when it was reopened as Bridgeview Grill, under the operation of Aramark, the company that was in charge of the university's dining services. The offerings were much different than the usual eateries at the university—filet bites with tobacco onion petals, blackened seafood fondue, rattlesnake shrimp with blue grits, strawberry salad, gorgonzola beef tenderloin and even a Belgian martini salad. The result for the Bridgeview Grill was the same as its predecessor, as easy, convenient parking was not available at the beautiful river location.

PART VIII

Make Us...International: The 1982 World's Fair

CHAPTER 22

ENERGY TURNS THE WORLD

THE SUNSPHERE RESTAURANT

A six-month-long party highlighting the beauty and resources of our area, the world is invited and every evening ends with fireworks and chicken dancing? Let's do it! East Tennessee completely embraced the 1982 World's Fair, with its theme song "You've got to be there, the 1982...World's...Fair!"

In the early 1970s, with the continual drain of business to the west side of town, downtown Knoxville needed a boost to jump-start redevelopment. Not merely a boost, but a so-called quantum leap. The idea for Knoxville to host a World's Fair was presented by W. Stewart Evans, then executive director of the Downtown Knoxville Association. Evans had heard how the 1974 World's Fair was already benefiting its host city of Spokane, Washington. He assessed the same could be done in Knoxville.

In 1975, the Downtown Knoxville Association requested that Mayor Kyle Testerman appoint a committee to conduct a feasibility study on Knoxville hosting a World's Fair. Testerman chose well-known young banker Jake Butcher as the head of the committee. The seventeen-member bipartisan committee of business, political and civic leaders reported back that the project was possible. Energy was suggested as the theme due to Knoxville's proximity to and association with the Oak Ridge National Laboratory and it being the headquarters of the Tennessee Valley Authority. The 1982 World's Fair, formally known as the Knoxville International Energy Exposition, was proposed to run from the beginning of May until the end of October with the theme "Energy Turns the World." In 1977, the fair was endorsed by President Jimmy Carter and the Tennessee General Assembly.

Enthusiasm for the fair grew and swelled all across the region. Then, It happened. In a throwback to the distasteful words of John Gunther, citing Knoxville as the ugliest city in America, in 1980 a reporter for the *Wall Street Journal* wrote a scathing article titled "What If You Gave a World's Fair and Nobody Came?" citing Knoxville as a "scruffy little city...on the Tennessee River." Shocked and appalled, but mostly hurt, the citizens of Knoxville banded together in their efforts. On May 1, 1982, President Ronald Reagan opened the Knoxville World's Fair with twenty-two different countries participating. Record attendance of 102,842 guests was set on October 9. On October 30, the day before the fair closed, the 11 millionth visitor passed through the gates.

Of course, you can't have a World's Fair without a theme structure. The fair management committee began working with William S. Denton, president of Community Tectonics Inc., and Hubert Bebb, the founder of that company, who had also been a designer at the 1933 World's Fair held in Chicago. Together they proposed the concept of the Sunsphere. The initial plan was for a glowing sphere, 160 feet tall, 86.5 feet in diameter, where five hundred guests could eat and drink on four revolving levels, at the projected cost of $3 million. The structure would serve as a symbol of the fair by representing the sun, the source of all energy. It would be a glowing beacon that would mark the fair site and would also serve as an observation tower.

The different levels of the sphere were meant to represent the formation of the earth through the ages and would be illustrated on each floor with sound systems, graphics, murals, furniture and color selections. The first floor was to be the Precambrian and Azoic era of rock dust and gas development, the second floor the rock and fossil development of the Precambrian and Proterozoic era, the third floor the age of fish of the Paleozoic era, the fourth floor the age of birds and dinosaurs of the Mesozoic era, the fifth floor the age of mammals or Cenozoic era and the sixth floor the future era of the space age.

The construction of the sphere would be of solar bronze glass, which would resemble the sun in the daytime, but in the evening it would give off a glow of a brilliant sunset. Preliminary plans included a call for two service elevators, two passenger elevators and two stairways. As the year went on, the projection for the height and the cost of the Sunsphere both increased.

When finished, the Sunsphere soared to be a 266-foot-tall steel truss structure, topped with a 75-foot gold-colored glass sphere. The glass-paneled windows were cut into seven different shapes and layered with twenty-four-carat gold dust. It weighed six hundred tons.

Sunsphere Restaurant ad. *McClung Historical Collection.*

During the fair, an observation deck was located on the first level of the sphere, the kitchen and private dining on level two, public dining rooms on levels three and four and a cocktail lounge on level five. An elevator was installed specifically for transporting product and kitchen supplies.

The Sunsphere Restaurant was run by the Specialty Food Service Division of Hardee's Food Systems, Inc., of Rocky Mount, North Carolina. Rolf Tinner, a native of Switzerland, was the executive chef. Hardee's did operate one of its signature fast-food franchises on the ground level near the Sunsphere, but the Sunsphere Restaurant was a fine dining establishment.

Fair visitors who wanted to ride the elevator up in the Sunsphere could purchase a ticket for two dollars, and then those who wanted to stay and dine would be assigned seats in the restaurant with the purchase of their elevator ticket. The third-floor dining room could seat 144 guests and the fourth floor 136. Hardee's executives estimated serving 2,000 guests a day.

Lunch and dinner in the main dining rooms featured items such as Rock Cornish game hen, prime rib, shrimp cocktail, Alaskan king crab legs and red snapper. A VIP dining room for visiting dignitaries could hold forty-eight and featured more elaborate meals of escargots, crab and lamb–stuffed mushrooms, beef wellington, chateaubriand, stuffed trout, rack of lamb, quail and even a tableside service of raspberry flambé baked Alaska.

In choosing the décor of the restaurant, it became apparent that the tint of the gold glass windowpanes changed the color of the fabrics. The wall coverings were in blue, while the carpet was sand, taupe and crimson, and the dining chairs were brushed satin chrome upholstered with a wine-colored fabric, except in the VIP lounge, where they were upholstered in deep blue with flecks of sand and red. Indirect lighting and candles on each table were meant to soften the atmosphere.

Designers of the uniforms for the workers at the restaurant also found working with color to be a challenge, noting that reds and blues looked good, but the gold glass turned brown and many other colors green. Judy Miler and Fann Burrus had heard that the Sunsphere Restaurant was looking for uniforms, and over a weekend, they worked up sketches and then presented them to the executives of Hardee's. A month later, they had produced prototypes in taupe, claret and navy. Hardee's hired them to produce 450 uniforms, which they did with other seamstresses in their homes. They produced khaki trousers and navy shirts for the elevator operators, taupe trousers with claret bow ties and vests to be worn with white shirts for waiters, taupe dresses belted and piped in claret for food waitresses, cowl-neck blouses with gathers on the shoulders and side-slit skirts linked by bronze belts for cocktail waitresses and sleeveless taupe sheath dresses with claret cummerbunds and boleros for hostesses.

The Sunsphere Restaurant was a big hit during the fair and served 400,000 guests. Food and drink totals included 207,998 shrimp, 90,998 prime rib, 37,792 red snapper, 19,611 orders of crab legs, 411,614 cheeseburgers, 603,553 French fries and 2,063 peanut butter and jelly sandwiches. In addition, 1,078,528 ounces of liquor were served. After the fair ended, Hardee's announced its intention to continue the fast-food establishment on the ground level, as well as the Sunsphere Restaurant.

The Blue Room opened on the fifth level of the sphere, while regular dining was on levels six and seven. The $2 elevator fee was still charged, but the restaurant would offset that cost by providing a free drink to diners. By 1983, the charge for the elevator was dropped, and free parking was touted across the way at Miller's. Although Hardee's had every intention of continuing the Sunsphere Restaurant, lack of promotion after the fair forced it to close in 1984, citing losing $1 million a year. Eighty-five people lost their jobs.

The Sunsphere then went dormant, but in a peculiar turn of events, the structure was referenced in 1996 in season 7, episode 20 of *The Simpsons*, "Bart on the Road," in which Bart makes a fake driver's license to take his friends on a spring break road trip. With a choice of Disney World or Knoxville, to the World's Fair, mentioned in an old guidebook, the gang chanted, "Knox-ville! Knox-ville! Knox-ville!" Upon arrival, they learned they were fourteen years too late. Asking about the Sunsphere, they receive the response, "You mean the Wigsphere?" as in this odd tale, the icon was being used to store sixteen thousand boxes of unsold wigs. Cute as the episode was, Knoxvillians are happy to note, "The Sunsphere is not a wig shop."

For a brief period in 1999, the observation deck was opened until the Public Building Authority made use of the space to oversee construction of the Knoxville Convention Center. In 2005, Mayor Bill Haslam, as part of his historic preservation initiatives, announced that the last two remaining structures created for the fair, the Sunsphere and the Tennessee Amphitheater, would be renovated and opened to the public. In 2007, an observation deck, free to the public, opened on the fourth floor, and then in 2008, privately owned businesses opened on the fifth, sixth, seventh and eighth floors.

CHAPTER 23

FAIR FOOD, A CANDY FACTORY AND A FOUNDRY

$\mathcal{A}$ lthough energy was the theme of the fair and was showcased along with daily world-class entertainment, oh, let's be honest, the majority of it was about eating. Eighty food vendors at the fair were allocated 200,000 square feet of operating space. All types of regional, national and international cuisine were offered.

Some national food brands were brought in as corporate sponsors and official products of the fair, including Stokely Van Camps, Stroh's Beer and Coca-Cola, which debuted flavored Coke products at the fair, including one that had much future success: Cherry Coke.

Knoxville-based companies were also official fair products and sponsors, including JFG Coffee, Kern's Bakery, Buddy's BBQ and Lay's Meats. Lay's had begun in Knoxville in 1913 as a retail meat market and later became a meat processor in 1920. In 1982, its processing plant covered two square blocks around Jackson Avenue in the Old City. Lay's products specifically used at the World's Fair were the hams that were hickory-smoked for fifteen hours, Ole Timer sausage, bacon, bologna, lunch meats, Touchdown franks and 3 Little Pigs wieners.

Pavilions of the different countries featured their native cuisine, such as the restaurant at the Hungarian pavilion, located right above the giant Rubik's cube. Beef goulash, rabbit paprika, stuffed cabbage rolls, chicken crepes and a dessert called palacintas—which was a crepe filled with currant jelly and then rolled in powdered sugar—pleased crowds. The Chinese pavilion featured hot and sour soup, spring rolls, chop suey, sweet and sour ribs, eggs rolls and fried rice. At the Korean pavilion, a restaurant was run by the Cha family, who owned a Korean restaurant in New York City called Arirang House along with two other restaurants in Seoul, Korea. They served pul koki (marinated and broiled sirloin), sam hap cho (sirloin tips and abalone) and sang sun chim (fried fish), among other traditional Korean dishes.

Located in the Mexican pavilion was the Fonda Santa Anita restaurant, chosen by the Mexican government to represent Mexico at World's Fairs in 1965 in New York, 1967 in Montreal, 1968 in San Antonio and 1982 in Knoxville. It was named as the best restaurant of the 1982 World's Fair by various newspapers, including the *Washington Post*. The owner, Arturo Guadalajara, only thirty-one years old, was a fourth-generation restaurateur. His great-grandfather opened the family's first restaurant in the 1800s in Mexico City. The Fonda Santa Anita was dedicated to preserving traditional Mexican cooking.

Arturo and his wife loved Knoxville so much that they stayed after the fair ended and moved the restaurant to a space in Homberg. Guests would be greeted with brightly patterned décor, hammered copper serving plates, the warmth of a fireplace and, for the women, a kiss on the hand. Mole poblano—chicken breasts simmered in fresh-ground chilies, raisins, almonds, bananas, sesame seeds, cumin, cinnamon and bitter chocolate— was their most popular dish of the fair and was offered along with other specialties, Mexican wines and beers and even a tangerine margarita. Although Arturo did not disclose his family recipes, he recommended the cookbook *Mexican Cuisine*, by Diana Kennedy, to guests interested in traditional Mexican cooking.

Beyond the new construction of the Sunsphere, amphitheater, lake and pavilions, planners were also making arrangements to incorporate historic structures of downtown into the fair. The reuse of the historical buildings was meant to represent true conservation of energy. World's Fair planners worked with the Tennessee Historical Commission and then Knoxville Heritage on redeveloping as many buildings as possible. The former Littlefield and Steere Candy Company, the remaining building of the Knoxville Iron Foundry and the old Louisville and Nashville Passenger and Freight Stations all housed eateries during the fair.

Littlefield and Steere began in the candy business in Knoxville in 1888 and became one of the largest candy manufacturers in the South. Mr. Steere had the distinction of being descended from a family who came over on the *Mayflower*. He and Mr. Littlefield came to Knoxville from Jacksonville, Florida, escaping an epidemic of yellow fever. They bought their first candy factory at a bargain, not knowing anything about the business, but learned as they went. Eventually, they specialized in stick candy, marshmallows, chocolates and bon bons, or what we would call today creams. The company operated out of two other locations on South Gay Street, at 262 and then 120, before building its third building in 1915 at 909 West Clinch Avenue, where it grew to 125 employees and was producing twenty thousand pounds of candy a day. The Littlefield and Steere Candy Company location at World's Fair Park became known as simply the Candy Factory.

During the fair, the terrace of the Candy Factory was outfitted as an Italian street festival with colorful umbrellas, mimes, acrobats and an organ grinder. Most of the food operations in the Candy Factory were run by Arie and Lisa Bos. The ground floor housed the Pasta Palace with its build-your-own pasta bar and Italian specialties. The second floor was L'Express— European fast foods. The third floor had the Expo Bar and Grill with seating for one hundred and a limited beef and seafood menu, plus a lavish Polynesian and French Canadian buffet for large groups. The Crow's Nest on the top floor was a Hawaiian-themed cocktail lounge with a fantastic view of the fairgrounds. Other offerings at the Candy Factory were a New York–style deli, Häagen-Dazs ice cream and See's Candies. The Boses also operated other food stands in the fair and hired three hundred employees to cover all their endeavors. Along with food, many arts and crafts were also showcased in the Candy Factory.

Elsewhere around the fair, two barges docked riverside featured a New Orleans–style seafood bar. The Garden Treats stand offered fried vegetables; House of Bacchus featured wine and cheese; Knackwurst Korner had knackwurst, bratwurst and Knoxville's favorite, mettwurst; and Brookhaven Farm served up country ham and sausage biscuits, pork chops, beans, corn bread and black walnut pie. There was Mother Hubbard's Cupboard of cookies and brownies, scratch-made desserts at Grandma's Cobbler, muffins covered in beef stew or other savory toppings at the Muffin Man, a Fresh Fruit Works stand and Petros, which went on to became a franchise throughout the Southeast. Brussels Patisserie offered doughnuts, cookies, crepes and my family's favorite, Belgian waffles, which could be topped with ice cream, fruit and whipped cream. Southern barbecued ribs, lox and bagels and Danish pastries and croissants were available. A stand called Skinny Dippers utilized potato skins in a Tom Sawyer theme. Huck Finn Thins were potato wedges dusted with parmesan cheese, Marco Twain was a pizza-type filling with mozzarella cheese and Nachos Queen featured chili and cheddar cheese.

Knoxville Iron Foundry, the last remaining building. *Brian Stansberry.*

Dips of sour cream with chives or horseradish and bacon or ketchup and parmesan could be added for dipping.

Along with all that variety, Filipino-, Japanese- and Caribbean-style cuisine, along with typical fair food of funnel cakes, cotton candy, popcorn, hot dogs, burgers, French fries, pizza, tacos, gyros, kabobs and fresh-squeezed lemonade, were available. In the midst of all that, the health conscious could find Sunfresh Salad Bar.

Also part of the fair site was the Knoxville Iron Foundry and Nail Factory, originally constructed around the late 1860s by brothers Joseph and David Richards and H.S. Chamberlain. David Richards and his teenage son, David John, had the unfortunate situation of being in the audience at Ford's Theater the night President Abraham Lincoln was shot. Richards had promised David John a trip to Washington upon passing his examinations at the Columbia Pennsylvania Classical and Military Institute. They recalled someone shouting, "The president has been shot!" followed by Mr. Ford announcing in a clear, loud voice with his hands uplifted, "John Wilkes Booth has shot the president, gone to the rear of the theater, mounted his horse and is on his way to the Long Bridge to go into Virginia." A few days later, the Richardses departed the city amid deep mourning and funeral dirges.

The Chamberlain, Richards & Co. complex originally contained seven buildings, including the foundry, a rolling mill for iron and a machine shop and mill for the railroad spike and nail production. The company employed 250 workers in the 1880s and grew to 850 employees in 1905. By the time of the fair, the foundry building was the only survivor of the complex.

Munich Festhaus was the name of the joint venture that would operate out of the Foundry during the fair, bringing authentic Bavarian food and entertainment to the site. However, the Festhaus sold so much Stroh's beer that it became known as the Strohaus. Servers carried ten mugs at a time to accompany popular German foods such as sauerbraten, various types of sausages, rotisserie chicken, potato dumplings, soups, breads and even eisbein (pig's knuckles). German bands played into the evening, and "chicken dancing" was encouraged.

Although the Strohaus was one of the most popular attractions of the fair, it made little profit. Munich Festhaus had invested $450,000 into the renovation of the building, had a weekly payroll of $30,000 and paid the German band $7,000 per week. After the fair ended, they reopened on November 5, hoping to make some money since all their bills had been paid. Along with many other fair businesses that planned to remain open after the fair ended, it closed shortly thereafter.

CHAPTER 24

DINING AT THE L&N STATION

The old Louisville and Nashville train station was greatly utilized during the fair. It was designed by Richard Montfort, the same architect who designed the Union Station in Nashville. Built in 1904, the station was influenced by the Chateaux and Beaux Arts styles of that time. It was used for passenger service up until 1968.

During the fair, the main lobby level of the L&N Station held the largest Ruby Tuesday's ever created, at 7,500 square feet, and the L&N Fish Market. Both restaurants were intended to complement, not compete with, each other. The L&N Fish Market was jointly operated by Greg Buschmohle and Alan Lamoureux, of Kansas City, and Ruby Tuesday. A large balcony overlooking the fair was shared by the two restaurants.

The L&N Fish Market received rave reviews. Fresh seafood was flown in every other day from Boston, and the kitchen was open, so guests could watch food being prepared. Specialties included fish charbroiled over mesquite wood, steamed clams, filet and crab legs, fried and broiled shrimp, lemon sole sauté, broiled lobster tail, linguini with white clam sauce, clam chowder and biscuits served in a skillet. Dinners were served with a salad of mixed greens and buttered potatoes. Strawberry torte and chocolate truffle cake were available for dessert.

After the fair, the name changed to L&N Seafood Grill, and the restaurant continued in operation much longer than many of the other fair eateries. It closed in 1993 because work on the Henley Street Connector cut off parking at the front entrance, causing business to drop 25 percent.

Louisville and Nashville passenger station. *Brian Stansberry.*

L&N Station rear stairway. *Brian Stansberry.*

L&N Station rear veranda. *Brian Stansberry.*

Management noted that in their customers' minds, there was no way to get in to the restaurant.

Pierre Interlude, a French restaurant run by Pierre Parker, also operated at the L&N. Parker was from Tours, France, where his entire family was in the restaurant business. His mother taught him her recipe for the famous soupe a l'oignon (French onion soup) that was served along with a special garlic bread in all-you-can-eat portions at the fair. The soup consisted of sausage and chicken stock combined with cognac and wine, topped with three different cheeses and croutons.

Parker had previously operated his restaurant in five World's Fairs: Seattle in '62, New York in '64–65, Montreal in '67, San Antonio in '68 and Spokane in '74. He felt the Knoxville World's Fair would be very successful because of the location and all the interesting places to visit nearby and additionally because Tennessee was so pretty and green.

In addition to the French onion soup, Parker offered cream Florentine, also an all-you-can-eat soup consisting of creamy spinach topped with hard-boiled, chopped eggs. Pâté de foie gras, crabmeat and fruit salads, snails

L&N freight depot. *Brian Stansberry.*

cooked in champagne and pastry and ice cream combinations flambé were also on the menu.

Although Parker had rented a house on Highland Avenue for the duration of the fair, his regular residence was in a large, rambling house in Carmel, California, purchased from actress Rita Hayworth. When asked what he did the rest of the time when not working at a World's Fair, Parker replied simply, "Nothing." Nothing…except planning and preparing for the next fair!

Even after the fair ended, the L&N continued to be one of the most utilized structures in the area. In 1996, Bruce Bogartz opened Southbound at the L&N, featuring upscale southern cuisine, before moving on to other ventures. In 2000, David Duncan opened the Jockey Club. His $400,000 investment restored the grandeur of the original main dining room of the train station. The restaurant was prix fixe fine dining in six courses. It closed in 2002.

On the lower level of the L&N freight depot, where fair souvenir shops had been, the Butcher Shop opened in 1993 and enjoyed a long run until closing in 2010. The Butcher Shop touted that its steaks were cooked by the best chef in the world—the customer—as they would be able to choose and prepare their own steak at brick charcoal pits. No matter the size or cut of the meat, the price was always the same, $9.95, and included a baked potato, French bread and a trip to the salad bar. The price was $1.00 extra if the house cooked the steak.

The Butcher Shop ad. *McClung Historical Collection.*

The closing of the Butcher Shop marked the end of restaurants at the L&N, as the STEM Academy, a high school through the Knox County School System dedicated to science, technology, engineering and math, was approved for the space.

The 1982 World's Fair was a great success for Knoxville. After the fair was over, proud East Tennesseans wore pins and T-shirts that exclaimed, "The Scruffy Little City Did It!"

The 1982 World's Fair—you had to be there.

PART IX

Visionaries

CHAPTER 25

ANNIE'S

BEGINNING A NEW "OLD CITY"

*Y*ou mean there's a place older than this?" my tour guests asked while crossing Gay Street after I mentioned the Old City. The term Old City can be somewhat confusing to newcomers. It is a misnomer, as the oldest part of Knoxville would be near the river. The name was created as a branding or marketing term for a particular area of town near Central and Jackson Avenues that actually developed around the 1850s, as the railroad was being built.

The expression "Old City" is attributed to Kristopher Kendrick and Patrick Roddy. Kendrick had a vision for this worn area of town that others couldn't imagine. When he mentioned to his friend and Coca-Cola Bottling Company owner Patrick Roddy that he had bought property on Jackson and Central with the intent of revitalizing the area, Roddy blatantly expressed, "Kris, that's the old city." The optimistic Kendrick replied, "Pat, that's the perfect name." And a new "Old City" was born.

"Don't you know what kind of neighborhood that is?" Kristopher Kendrick remembered his father saying. "Pop, I'm going to change it," Kendrick replied. Once restoration began and new businesses started opening, nearly every article or mention of that particular part of town thereafter noted, "They prefer to call it the Old City." Intrigued about what was being imagined in this previously run-down neighborhood, locals followed suit with the language.

The Old City became one of our favorite destinations in college. Rummaging through vintage stores in old warehouses was a favorite

The Old City, with Manhattan's on the right. *Brian Stansberry.*

Saturday afternoon pastime. The Old City was an outlet for the creative, the alternative and the inspired. It was a getaway, an escape, an area of Knoxville where you could feel like you were somewhere much cooler than Knoxville and that you were even a much cooler version of yourself. Filled with old abandoned brick warehouses, industrial buildings and the massive railyard, the Old City had been the perfect hideout for outlaws and outsiders and now artists, musicians and restless young people. It was restored just enough to feel safe but left alone just enough to feel edgy.

Many eclectic eateries and clubs have passed through the Old City: Manhattan's; Spaghetti Warehouse; Old City Grill; New City Café; JFG Coffeehouse; Amigo's; Black Sheep Café; Pasta Trio; Summit Diner at the corner of Central and Summit Hill; El Camino; the vegetarian All Night Eggplant, which did not serve eggplant all night; and, in the words of one of my tour guests, "What about Ella Guru's?"

But before all those, one of the first proponents of the Old City in the 1980s was Annie DeLisle, formerly Annie McCarthy. She lived in one of the condominiums renovated by Kristopher Kendrick. After her mother passed away, she asked Kendrick what he would do next, if he were her and could do whatever he wanted and be whoever he wanted to be. Kendrick answered that he would open a little restaurant in the Old City, something unlike anything anyone had ever seen in town.

Right: Manhattan's ad/menu. *McClung Historical Collection.*

Below: Jackson Avenue skyline view from Southern Railway Station (*front*). Also seen are JFG Coffee Headquarters (*left*) and the Sterchi Brothers Furniture building (*right*). *Brian Stansberry.*

"Well, there was this place we would go in the Old City, it had a woman's name," my friend related. "Oh, Annie's," I told her. "She was the ex-wife of Cormac McCarthy," I threw in for special effect. "Really!?" she responded, immediately recognizing the name of the Pulitzer Prize–winning author. Annie, the English-born ballet dancer, came to Knoxville following their marriage.

Annie's—A Very Special Restaurant opened at 106 North Central in 1983 with twenty investors. I have a feeling that—just as at the Atlanta Bazaar in *Gone with the Wind*, "If Melanie Wilkes says it's alright, it tis alright"—if Annie DeLisle said it was a very special restaurant, then it was a very special restaurant.

Guests were to look for the entrance near the only dogwood tree on Central Avenue, as the restaurant was not marked with a sign. It was a small gray stucco building connected to Patrick Sullivan's. Inside, twelve tables would seat twenty-eight guests. The first chef was Micael de Burca. That's Mee-haal to us. Annie had met him while he was working as chef of Piccolo's at the Pembroke.

Dinner at Annie's—A Very Special Restaurant included an appetizer, bread and butter, salad or soup, entrée, dessert and coffee at a prix fixe of $13.95. Now it's my turn to say, Really!? Although, one of Micael's signature dishes—fusilli pasta with cream, white wine, strawberries and Italian truffles—had a $3.50 surcharge because of the extra expense of the truffles. Another extravagance of Micael's was Sundae a la Maison—ice cream covered with green, red and blue grapes, as well as strawberries and blueberries, topped with a chocolate Cognac sauce that used a Swiss semisweet chocolate that sold for $20.00 a pound.

Piccolo's at the Pembroke menu. *McClung Historical Collection.*

The prix fixe increased to $17.95 in 1986 but still featured lush dishes of rich and creamy almond soup, light and cool chilled watercress soup, salads of fresh greens with tart dressings, Dover sole covered with a chive sauce and key lime fusilli with shrimp and scallops. By 1988, lack of easy parking in the Old City began hurting business at Annie's as other restaurants and bars were opening and more people were coming to experience the revitalized area. When Annie opened her restaurant in the Old City, there was nothing else going on in the area. By 1989, there were twenty-nine businesses. Although Annie said those six years were among the most fabulous of her life, she decided to close in 1989, relating that she was very, very tired.

Mark Wischhusen had been a patron of Annie's and was a part owner of the Blues Harbor club in Atlanta. He took over the space and reopened as Lucille's, a restaurant and jazz club, named for his mother. He closed Lucille's in 1996, but it was revived by Frank Gardner in 2001 as part of Patrick Sullivan's. Gardner created Back Room BBQ in the space before closing in 2011.

The building was not of the best construction and had fallen into bad condition. In 2013, there began to be calls to demolish the worn structure. Later, the space became the outdoor patio of Tim Love's Love Shack, adjacent to his Lonesome Dove Bistro. But we can always remember, once upon a time, that small space was home to—a very special restaurant.

CHAPTER 26

T. HO'S VIETNAMESE AMERICAN DREAM

Thanh Ho escaped communist Vietnam with his wife and six children in a thirty-six-foot-long wooden fishing boat along with seventy-nine other refugees in 1980. They had all spent years making the preparations. Although they knew many had died trying to escape, they were willing to risk the twelve-day trip to the Philippines. The group took turns bailing water from their boat in fifty-minute intervals. The day after they landed, the boat was destroyed by a typhoon. A few years later, Thanh "T." Ho opened the first Vietnamese restaurant in Knoxville.

Luckily, Thanh had a relative in Knoxville, which gave him and his family sponsorship. Upon their arrival in Knoxville, Thanh could not speak English but learned quickly through a government-sponsored program. He became a U.S. citizen in the 1980s and even graduated from State Technical Institute, now Pellissippi State Technical Community College, as an electronics technician. However, the real dream of Thanh and his wife, On Dang, upon arrival in America was to open their own business. They didn't know what it would be until their new American friends started tasting, and raving over, On Dang's egg rolls.

In 1986, On Dang and Thanh opened a carry-out on Broadway, while Thanh still worked a full-time job as an electronics technician. A year later, they opened T. Ho Vietnamese and Oriental Restaurant at 815 Merchants Drive, in North Knoxville.

T. Ho quickly became popular for its Vietnamese specialties, beginning with the egg rolls or spring rolls and On Dang's sauce of tomato, garlic and sweet rice. The rolls were in a crisp wrapper filled with pork, shrimp or chicken and vegetables, including carrots. My guests and I ate many of these during my tours. I began to notice I kept hearing at various restaurants around town, "The spring roll from T. Ho," or, "T. Ho's spring roll" being presented. They were being sold through a distributor to area restaurants, which loved featuring them as a local product.

The family started their packaged foods factory, T. Ho Foods, in 1996, offering the rolls in packages of four, pork patties, T. Ho Nuoc Mam sauce (a light vinegar-based sauce sweetened with pineapple juice and sugar) and customized products for restaurants. All the spring rolls were assembled by hand and were not precooked. As well as being offered in local restaurants, they were picked up by area grocery stores, one manager noting the quality, packaging and cost of the product as excellent. The majority of the marketing was by word of mouth.

Other specialties at T. Ho were the Vietnamese crepes, grilled meatballs and noodles with pork, beef, chicken or shrimp. The Vietnamese crepe was a French-influenced dish, a rice flour omelet filled with shrimp, chicken, mushrooms, onions and bean sprouts served with cucumber, lettuce, pickled carrots and the Nuoc Mam sauce. The grilled meatballs were sliced and added to raw vegetables and then wrapped in rice paper. Steamed vermicelli rice noodles on a bed of lettuce with marinated sweet carrots and cucumbers topped with the guest's choice of meat stir fried, then sprinkled with peanuts, made up the noodle dish.

In 2006, T. Ho underwent a major remodel and was revamped to T. Ho Bistro Fresh Vietnamese Kitchen. With the influx of upscale Asian restaurants, the family felt an urge to move from a family-type atmosphere to something more ambient. Hardwood floors and track lighting were added in the dining room, along with new tables and chairs with sewed charcoal-colored cushions. Fresh paint added a red wall and a moss green wall, and the kitchen was doubled in size. Wine was added to the menu. That same year, Thanh's sons opened the Pint House adjoining T. Ho, focusing on the trendy beer craze.

T. Ho Bistro closed in 2007, but the sons revived it again in 2016 as T. Ho Fresh Vietnamese Kitchen. The revival of T. Ho lasted less than a year, but the Pint House continued serving up those famous T. Ho spring rolls.

Though they had survived many hardships—war, work camp, the death of two children, a harrowing escape and a longing for home in a place where the landscape looked a lot like their own—Thanh and On Dang enjoyed the opportunity to achieve success in America. Thanh related that he felt that he was the luckiest man in the world here.

CHAPTER 27

GONE TOO SOON

KENNY SIAO, MANGO AND CHA CHA

B ig changes were in store for Knoxville in the 1990s, when the cable television network Home and Garden Television started up. HGTV became part of the E.W. Scripps Company, which separated into two companies, E.W. Scripps and Scripps Networks Interactive, headquartered in Knoxville, which produced the Food Network, the Travel Channel, the DIY Network, the Cooking Channel and more.

In the 1990s, restaurateur Kenny Siao was on the cutting edge of our culinary world with his whimsical Mango, Cha Cha Tapas Bar and the popular Stir Fry Café. By 2004, he was gone, tragically drowned on a beach trip at age forty-three.

Siao came to Knoxville from Malaysia in 1981 to study at the University of Tennessee. He graduated with a degree in civil engineering in 1985. Siao owned a restaurant called SanPan in Gatlinburg, but in 1993, he opened Stir Fry Café at 7240 Kingston Pike, serving exotic, spicy dishes from his homeland. Siao said the idea for Stir Fry was to be like a place you would find in Knoxville's Old City, with patio seating, jazz and blues bands and the atmosphere of an art gallery, but in West Knoxville, where plentiful parking was easily available. I now understand the Stir Fry Café. The food was to be Thai and Oriental.

The Stir Fry Café was quite successful, prompting Siao to open Mango, at 5803 Kingston Pike, in 1999. Mango was a flight of fancy, a bright spot of color, a getaway right on Kingston Pike that gave folks a real yearning to dine out. It fit right into the chic Bearden District.

The Asian-Caribbean menu was designed by chef Dean Holsberry. Siao called it cross-cultural cuisine.

The intriguing menu at Mango consisted of appetizers such as tuna tartare with a saki wasabi vinaigrette, Thai lobster roll with nouc cham dressing, calamari tempura with an apricot glaze and green curry chutney and Szechuan pork quesadillas with papaya salsa. Entrées included kiwi-glazed halibut with a saki mandarin orange sauce; pan-seared jumbo scallops with squid ink pasta and lemon caper cream sauce; and seared duck breast with guava glaze and cinnamon–sweet potato strudel. Buffalo osso buco on cheese polenta, bouillabaisse and roasted pork loin stuffed with apricots and raisins with a tomato bacon vinaigrette were later additions, as well as an eight-compartment Japanese bento box. The signature dessert at Mango was a "smokeless" dense truffle cake in the shape of a cigar, served on a crystal ashtray with cappuccino ice cream and "ashes." Other desserts included a banana burrito with white chocolate in a phyllo crust with rum raisin ice cream, candied ginger cream brûlée, a tiramisu cheesecake, pumpkin muffins with Wild Turkey cream sauce and mango sorbet with fresh fruit and a sugar cookie.

"We used to eat at Cha Cha a lot," my recent tour guests unexpectedly remarked to me. "Oh, Cha Cha, we did too!" I remembered. Siao opened his cutting-edge Cha Cha Tapas Bar in 2001 at 5130 Kingston Pike, in the Homberg area of Bearden. Siao once remarked that people said Knoxvillians wouldn't try anything new, but he disagreed, noting, "The population will try anything." Asked about the name, Siao replied, "It's fun like a dance, and I do like a dance."

The contemporary design of the restaurant featured colorful pieces of broken tile, miniature fiber optic lights along a concrete bar and stylized chandeliers of steel ribbons. A community dining table was available for those wanting to socialize and make new friends while eating, which Siao noted that people loved.

Twenty-four different tapas were on the menu, ranging in price from $4.50 to $7.00. Shrimp ceviche served in a martini glass, duck confit with cellophane noodles and bacon-wrapped sea bass were popular tapas, while grilled pork tenderloin with veggie mashed potatoes accompanied by chorizo gravy and squash fries and vegetarian or seafood, chicken and sausage paella were available as entrées. The warm Spanish chocolate cake with an oozing filling and vanilla bean ice cream was recommended for dessert. A best-selling drink at Cha Cha was the Flirtini, composed of vodka, raspberry liqueur, triple sec, cranberry juice and pineapple juice shaken and served in a martini glass with a splash of champagne floating on top. The frothy, pink drink was similar to a Cosmopolitan, made so famous by the popular television series of the time, *Sex and the City*.

In 2004, Siao opened a second Stir Fry Café in Johnson City with partners Ned Vickers, Robert Talbott and Mark Shipe. Shipe noted that Siao was a very smart businessman and had an "out-of-this-world" charisma about him. He went on to say that Siao was a great visionary and had class and taste that money couldn't buy.

After the shocking news of Siao's passing, his family vowed to keep his restaurants going. They wanted to preserve Siao's legacy and did not want "his inspiration, spirit and idealism to die with him." It was noted that the restaurants were making money and should continue operations as usual. Over time, Siao's family, who ran a marketing firm in Malaysia and had no prior experience in the restaurant business, sold the establishments to locals.

Dean Holsberry, the chef who had designed the original menu, bought Mango. It closed in 2006. Cha Cha was bought by Bill Robinson, the former international director of operations for Ruby Tuesday, and his wife, Janet. They had fallen in love with Cha Cha and, after hearing it was up for sale, made an offer the following day. The Robinsons made changes of an expanded menu, lower price points and more entrées. They also incorporated a children's menu. The Robinsons closed Cha Cha in 2007, noting a downturn in the economy. Stir Fry Café continued at its original location on Kingston Pike; the Johnson City location closed, and a new Stir Fry opened in Kingsport, Tennessee.

The Mango location became Le Parigo and then Seth Simmerman's Echo after Le Parigo moved downtown and eventually closed. Cha Cha became the Bearden location of Nama Sushi Bar in 2008.

Kenny Siao, daring risk-taker—it was said his restaurants represented his personality. Thank you for including Knoxville in your dance.

PART X

Turn the Page: Downtown Revival Pioneers

CHAPTER 28

MAHASTI, SCOTT AND LULA'S ROLE IN REDEVELOPMENT

While the 1990s were definitely a high point for restaurants in the Bearden District, the 2000s were bringing a shift back to, of all places, downtown Knoxville. Back to where it all started. Unless you worked downtown, you were probably not used to going to downtown Knoxville. To suburbanites, it was desolate, deserted and even a bit scary. There were three restaurants that took me on a trip out of my comfort zone of West Knoxville to the downtown area. The first one was Lula, opened by the husband-and-wife team of Mahasti Vafaie and Scott Partin exactly for that purpose.

Mahasti was born in Iran, but when she was a teenager, during the time of the revolution, her parents moved her to Murfreesboro, Tennessee, to live with her sister, who was studying at Middle Tennessee State University. She later became a naturalized United States citizen. After graduating with a mechanical engineering degree from the University of Tennessee, Mahasti moved to Mississippi to work at an oil well servicing company. Seeing how women didn't have the same opportunities as men in Iran, growing up Mahasti always wanted to be employed. After nine months, she decided to return to UT to study pre-med.

It was on a vacation to New Orleans with her mother that Mahasti found her true calling. While they were in a café there, Mahasti read a newspaper article about the woman who opened the establishment. Inspired by the story, she decided then that was what she wanted to do. Back in Knoxville, she leased a space at 12 Market Square to open the Flying Tomato in 1990 as something new and different for the city. The Flying Tomato became the very successful Tomato Head. But it wasn't an easy start.

Tomato Head was open for lunch, just like most of the other downtown restaurants of that time, for the downtown workers. To get by in the beginning, Mahasti worked at other restaurants too. She would work at Tomato Head until it closed in the afternoon at 2:00 p.m., then head off to a serving job at another restaurant. For four years, she worked seventeen-hour days, without a paycheck from Tomato Head. When she extended her operation to evening hours at Tomato Head, she got by on tips she earned while serving. She credits the loyal clientele from the downtown office of Whittle Communications as helping them through their first few years.

University of Tennessee student Chris Whittle got his start producing a student guide called *Knoxville in a Nutshell* with his friends out of an old pillow factory in South Knoxville. In 1979, they bought struggling *Esquire* magazine and turned it around. By 1986, the company had become Whittle Communications, with six hundred employees, twenty-one magazines and annual revenue of $75 million. By 1988, Whittle Communications had grown to nine hundred employees, and in 1992, it moved into its new 250,000-square-foot neo-Georgian headquarters building in downtown Knoxville. Citing various financial difficulties, the company ceased operations in 1994, and the building became a federal courthouse.

Mahasti and her husband, Scott, decided to open another restaurant on Market Square in an effort to draw more people to the downtown area. In 1998, Lula, in the Southwest style, opened at 24 Market Square. Other restaurants on the Square at the time were the Soup Kitchen; Gus's, which operated out of the old Peroulas/Gold Sun location; Café Max; Subway; and Papa John's.

Design for the space was done by Sparkman Architects. Much work had to be done on the building, which was damaged from neglect. New oak floors were put in, as well as a new roof. Handmade oak tables, chairs and bar counters were brought in from Asheville. Blue was used at the entrance, as in Mexican and other cultures, the color blue is thought to ward off evil spirits. The design and décor was simple and understated to allow the food to shine. The space also featured an open kitchen, visible from the dining area.

Mahasti was dedicated to continued learning in her craft and traveled to study food and cooking with chefs in restaurants around the country. She worked briefly at two restaurants in San Francisco, Greens and Café Marimba, the latter of which had been voted the city's best Mexican

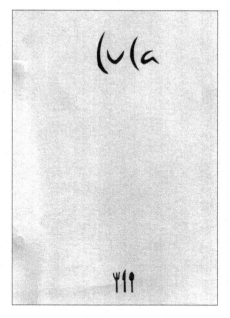

Lula menu. *Scott Partin.*

restaurant for several years running, and then at celebrity chef Rick Bayless's Frontera Grill in Chicago. Later, she studied with Diana Kennedy, the leading authority on authentic Mexican cuisine. Mahasti even taught classes of her own at the University of Tennessee in enchilada and burrito preparation.

The cuisine at Lula was to be Mexican with a California flair, with handmade corn tortillas, authentic Mexican sauces and marinades and lots of fresh vegetables. The menu consisted of specialties such as the Lula chimichanga with chicken, spinach, potatoes, manchego cheese, red onions and a pasilla chile mole. Other favorites were the portabella mushroom enchilada or portabella pasta, avocado shrimp pasta, chicken mole salad, various burritos, quesadillas, tomato mint salsa and Veracruz pasta with shrimp, olives, capers and fresh tomatoes served with angel hair pasta. A fruit guacamole, adapted from Diana Kennedy, was made from avocado, jalapeño, onion, garlic, peaches, grapes and mango. For dessert, Mahasti made cheesecake, while Scott made chocolate soufflé cake and flan. The tres leches cake was infused with three kinds of milk and served with rich caramelized banana slices.

During the time Mahasti and Scott were running Lula, part of an old brick wall collapsed in on the south side of Tomato Head, causing major

BURRITOS
Served with chef's choice side item and crema

Steak Burrito
Ancho Seasoned Steak, basmati rice, spinach, roasted red onion, fresh tomato salsa and manchego cheese
$9.95

Chicken Burrito
Chicken, roasted corn, roasted peppers and roasted red onion, basmati rice and manchego cheese
$8.95

Hot Burrito #1
Chicken, black beans, red onion, pickled jalapeño, cilantro, basmati rice and chipotle crema
$8.95

Bean and Rice Burrito
Refried beans, basmati rice, roasted corn, roasted tomato and manchego cheese
$6.95

Pineapple Walnut Burrito
Baked tofu, black beans, walnuts, fresh spinach, roasted red onion, cilantro, goat cheese and grilled pineapple salsa
$8.95

Veggie Burrito
Fresh spinach, guacamole, roasted red onion, roasted artichoke hearts, herbed cream cheese and fresh tomato salsa served cold
$8.95

Scallop Burrito
Seared Scallops, spinach, rice and chipotle cream sauce
$9.95

Tofu Burrito
Baked tofu, roasted artichoke hearts, fresh spinach, basmati rice, black beans, manchego cheese and spicy chipotle salsa
$8.95

BEAN AND RICE BOWLS
Basmati rice topped with choice of black or refried beans, crema and the ingredients listed below. Served with crisp flour tortilla triangles

Salsa Bowl
Fresh tomato salsa
$4.95

Guacamole Bowl
Guacamole and fresh tomato salsa
$6.95

Fajita Bowl
Fresh spinach, roasted corn and fajita seasoned tofu and veggies
$6.95

Chicken Bowl
Grilled chicken in mole, guacamole, manchego cheese and fresh tomato salsa
$7.95

Pineapple Bowl
Baked Tofu, walnuts and grilled pineapple salsa
$7.95

SOUP
Weekly selection
cup $1.95 \ bowl $3.95

SALADS
House Salad
Romaine lettuce with carrots, mushrooms, red cabbage and red onion.
$3.95

Grilled Caesar Salad
Romaine lettuce grilled and served with caesar dressing
$5.95

Chicken Salad
Grilled chicken, avocado and red onion on a bed of Romaine lettuce, carrots, mushrooms and red cabbage.
$6.95

Tofu Salad
Baked Tofu, avocado and red onion on a bed of Romaine lettuce, carrots, mushrooms and red cabbage.
$6.95

dressings:
Balsamic Lime Vinaigrette
Creamy Cilantro Garlic
Caesar

PASTA
Scallop Pasta
Seared Scallops and spinach in a mushroom cream sauce. Served over fettuccine and topped with parmesan cheese.
$13.95

Artichoke Pasta
Chicken, fresh spinach, mushrooms, roasted artichoke hearts, red onion and tomato in a pasilla cream sauce. Served over fettuccine and topped with manchego cheese.
$11.95

ENCHILADAS
Fresh filled corn tortillas covered in mole and crema and baked. Served with cilantro rice cake and seasonal vegetable.

Chicken Enchilada
Chicken, fresh spinach, roasted red onion and manchego cheese
$10.95

Spinach Enchilada
Black beans, fresh spinach and goat cheese topped with pickled red onion
$9.95

Cheese Enchilada
Manchego cheese, goat cheese, fresh spinach and roasted red onion
$10.95

Tofu Enchilada
Baked Tofu and manchego cheese
$9.95

CHIMICHANGAS
Fried burrito topped with mole and topped with pickled red onions and crema.

Chicken Chimichanga
Chicken, basmati rice, manchego cheese and fresh spinach
$9.95

Steak Chimichanga
Ancho seasoned steak, basmati rice, roasted red onion and manchego cheese
$9.95

Tofu Chimichanga
Tofu, black beans, basmati rice, fresh spinach and manchego cheese
$8.95

DESSERT
Flan
$3.95

Chocolate Bread Pudding with chocolate sauce
$5.95

Summer Berry Pudding with whipped cream
$4.95

Rice Empanada
flour tortilla filled with rice pudding with mango cream
$5.95

Tres Leches
Sponge cake infused with three milks and served with deglazed seasonal fruit
$6.95

COFFEE / TEA
Espresso $1.25
Cappuccino $2.00
Latte $2.50
Pot of Coffee $2.00
Pot of Tea $2.00

Above and left: Lula menu. *Scott Partin.*

structural damage. The space had to be closed temporarily. Knoxville's favorite godfather appeared again to tell us just what should happen. Kristopher Kendrick relayed that he was "horrified to learn of the damage" and offered up a temporary space in the Peter Kern building across the Square, noting that "Mahasti is a wonderful person who has a good business. If she can use this space to keep the Tomato Head going, she's welcome to move over here and just pay the utility bill."

Despite rave reviews, Lula closed in 2000. The closure of Lula took many by surprise. The shuttering of such a beautiful concept simply because not enough people were coming downtown really got people thinking about a plan for the redevelopment of Market Square. The president of the Knoxville Area Chamber Partnership met with Mahasti and Scott to see what could be done. He related that if they couldn't create a new business with their track record of quality and service, it would be difficult for anyone to open a new business downtown. Lula's closing was a dramatic illustration of what a downtown plan was all about—producing a mix of residents and workers to sustain businesses long term.

Back to focusing all their energy on Tomato Head, that flying tomato really soared. Mahasti's dream became a reality. In 2002, the city council approved an $8.8 million resurrection of Market Square by Kinsey Probasco & Associates of Chattanooga. So it just might have been another dream, that short-lived, understated southwestern jewel, Lula, that really made it possible for Tomato Head and other restaurants that followed on Market Square to succeed. Here's to Lula. Is it time for a reprise?

CHAPTER 29

THE CRESCENT MOON CAFÉ

I had read about the Crescent Moon Café and was intrigued enough to again make my way downtown, navigate the one-way streets and find parking. The café was started in the mid-1990s by Terri Korom and Michelle Berry, who met at a party after moving to Knoxville and opened a restaurant and catering business together two weeks later. Michelle was originally from Boston but had been a pastry chef at the Watergate Hotel in Washington, D.C., before she discovered East Tennessee on a hiking trip in the Smokies and decided to stay. Terri was from Clearwater, Florida, and chose Knoxville randomly on a map as a sort of retreat and place to "quit doing drugs." She never told anyone she was leaving Florida. Once here, she worked as a graphic artist, journeyman sign painter, photographer and event planner before opening the restaurant.

The Crescent Moon Café was operated out of a basement at 705 Market Street for seven years, during which time Terri won the Massachusetts Mutual Blue Chip award for healthy foods. She was focused on low-fat dishes using lots of fresh herbs and very little salt. Everything was made on site, even the salad dressings. The restaurant could cater to those with heart problems or diabetes. In 1999, the Crescent Moon was featured in *Nation's Business* magazine as a small business that overcame adversity to reach the pinnacle of success. Terri noted that running a downtown business was a struggle but still the most fun thing she had ever done.

One of the best-selling menu items at the Crescent Moon was the Fungi and Mold, a tortilla filled with Swiss cheese, portabella mushrooms brushed with red wine vinaigrette, tofu and a garlic dill spread. The wrap was so popular that patrons would call ahead to order it for lunch. The name was chosen by a contest. Downtown diners also loved Terri's smoked turkey roll-up, burgundy mushroom soup and crispy seared tuna on sesame noodles. Her food was so well liked that it prompted the *Crescent Moon Cookbook*.

Terri's Recipe for Herbed Potato Casserole

10 small red potatoes
1 tablespoon fresh rosemary
1 tablespoon fresh basil
2 small zucchini, sliced
2 small yellow squash, sliced
2 stalks celery, chopped
½ cup chopped red onions
5 cloves garlic, roasted and minced
Crushed red pepper to taste
1 cup fat-free yogurt
Croutons
Parmesan or shredded cheddar cheese

Boil potatoes with herbs until soft. Drain and cut into cubes or quarters for small potatoes.

Sauté vegetables with garlic and red pepper.

Spoon potatoes in bottom of a large baking dish. Layer with yogurt, then veggies. Top with croutons and cheese to taste.

Bake at 300 degrees for 40 minutes.

Yield: 6 to 8 servings

Terri was very involved with the downtown community and participated in events such as the Women's Expo. She also cooked and provided food for charitable events for many local organizations.

In 2002, Terri planned to move the Crescent Moon out of its basement location to Market Square in the space that had been used by Tomato Head while its collapsed wall was being repaired. By the time I found the eatery, she had found a different location, at 718 South Gay Street, the former home of Salsa Café and Bullfeathers. Here Terri continued with healthy salads, sandwiches, wraps and fresh vegetables.

One of the best and most memorable meals that I've ever had in a Knoxville restaurant, or a restaurant anywhere, was at the Crescent Moon. I don't know why I chose to order what I thought was a simple bowl of mashed potatoes and corn that day. I had no idea that potatoes were one of Terri's specialties. That, in fact, they sold out of potatoes every day. In addition to potatoes and corn, Terri offered other combinations of potatoes and carrots, spinach, broccoli, beets, horseradish, parmesan and garlic or other spices. Her method was to cook the vegetables together, then mash them at the same time. Another technique was to use sour cream, half and half, cream cheese or yogurt instead of or in addition to milk.

After closing the Crescent Moon Café in 2003, Terri continued catering and worked as a food coordinator for a program on the DIY Network. She continued her outreach in the community by offering a Kids in the Kitchen program and cooking for the YWCA through a program with St. John's Cathedral. A downtown pioneer—we're glad Terri picked Knoxville.

CHAPTER 30

LA COSTA

GREG WHITE'S GREEN DREAM

*L*a Costa on Market Square. La Costa should have stayed. I viewed it as the beginning of our new downtown. It was in the Latin style, so popular in Knoxville, featuring young chefs full of fresh new ideas. The new Market Square parking garage was finished, and you could come out of the garage right near the restaurant, providing a solution to any West Knoxvillians' apprehensions about dining downtown. I still remember the first time a friend said to me, "Oh, I think we can just park at the garage, at Market Square." Park at the garage at Market Square? We were all trying to grasp this new concept.

Greg White had opened his groundbreaking Nama Sushi Bar downtown in 2004, on the 100 block of Gay Street. He was later inspired by his two-year-old daughter, Emma Claire, to set a good example for her by living environmentally consciously. This inspiration resulted in White opening his second restaurant in 2006, which became the eco-friendly eatery La Costa at 31 Market Square.

In 2007, La Costa received a Green Certification from the Green Restaurant Association. It was only the second restaurant in Tennessee to earn the honor. Many steps went into being a green restaurant, including using a comprehensive recycling system for waste products, using products free of Styrofoam and a commitment to completing four environmentally friendly steps every year.

White invested in a truck and trailer to take glass, paper, metal, aluminum and plastic to the recycling center every week. All paper products such as menus, paper towels, take-out containers and office paper were either biodegradable, compostable or made from other recycled products. Compact fluorescent lighting, which could last twelve times longer, was used rather than ordinary bulbs. All cleaning supplies were non-toxic and chlorine free, and low-flow aerators were used on the sinks to conserve water. Cooking oil was recycled, and locally grown, organic vegetables were primarily used. The beef and chicken were free-range, the seafood was non-farmed and even the wine offered at La Costa was organic and from 100 percent self-sustaining vineyards. Going green caused a 4 to 6 percent increase in operating costs, but White expected to save money on water and utilities. With his staff dedicated to the idea as well, White related that La Costa had become "greener than I thought we could ever achieve."

The food at La Costa was to be nuevo-latino cuisine with a fresh twist. It was described as "a fun new place to eat on Market Square." The atmosphere was simple and sleek. Walls and the ceiling were washed in shades of soft blue, green and brown. Wooden tables and slatted-back chairs followed by booths lined the left of the space along a natural brick wall, while a bar with a long wine rack was immediately to the right. Paintings from local artists hung on the walls.

White and Chef Brandon Cruze developed a menu committed to natural, organic, fresh, seasonal and local ingredients. Early menu items included small plates of grilled flank steak or fish tacos and entrées such as tempura eggplant napoleon; braised short rib of beef on plantain blini with buffalo oysters and cucumber salsa; goat cheese and roasted red pepper quesadilla; red curry with tofu; and jerk-rubbed salmon with roasted corn and mashed potatoes with a sweet pea coulis. With the first bite, I proclaimed it my new favorite restaurant.

La Costa was a small restaurant with no walk-in cooler, only a three-door cooler. There was no space to make big batches or to store premade items, guaranteeing the consumer their product would be made fresh. The menu only continued to evolve and later featured starters of a salad of orange supremes, julienned fennel and shaved radishes with an orange cumin vinaigrette; brie en croute with citrus marmalade, chipotle candied pecans and tortilla points; and scallop and shrimp ceviche with tomatillos, red onion, corn, sherry vinegar and blackened tortilla points. Entrées included roast bone-in pork chops with Benton's bacon corn pudding and sautéed Brussels sprouts; beef culotte with peppered fig sauce, blue cheese Yukon mashed potatoes and pan-roasted broccolini; and pan-seared grouper with Spanish rice, braised Swiss chard and a blood orange coulis. Desserts were a phyllo-wrapped banana with walnuts, chocolate and coconut Chantilly; ginger panna cotta with raspberry gelée and white chocolate crème Anglaise; and the unforgettable white chocolate Blondie with pumpkin ice cream.

In 2008, White sold La Costa to Ken and Mary Carol Eddleman of Atlanta in order to return his focus to Nama. That same year, he opened the second location of Nama at 5130 Kingston Pike in Bearden, along with Emma's at Choto Marina. White's idea was to take the concept of Nama to hotels, and he planned to open one in the Westin north of Orlando, Florida. In 2011, he planned a new restaurant and bar at the corner of Jackson Avenue and Broadway, to be called the Corner BP. Those projects did not work out, and White eventually sold Nama and moved on to other interests.

Although La Costa closed in 2011, Greg White's eclectic eatery played a major role in drawing more of the Knoxville population downtown. White's advice to restaurateurs wanting to be environmentally friendly was to be "100 percent dedicated to the cause. You have to think about it daily. You have to plan. You have to seek out ways. You have to be creative, and you have to have above all else a staff that believe in the same things you do." La Costa, on Market Square.

Greg White, along with the many other past restaurateurs of Knoxville, was not out for riches or fame but to bring something new, creative and of quality to his city. It has been a pleasure and honor learning and preserving their stories.

BIBLIOGRAPHY

CHAPTER 1

Blount, William. *William Blount Letters*, December 17, 1795.

Bowman, James S. "Evidence Relating to the Location of John Chisholm's Tavern." June 3, 1948.

Brown, Lucia. "Dilapidated Chisholm Tavern Goes On." *Knoxville Journal*, August 1, 1937.

Cunningham, Bob. "Chisholm's Tavern Isn't, But…" *Knoxville News Sentinel*, June 16, 1957.

Durman, Louise. "Vintage Victuals Food of Blount Era to Be Demonstrated." *Knoxville News Sentinel*, March 13, 1991.

Godfrey, Mrs. Elmore. "It's Knoxville Obligation to Save Tavern." *Knoxville News Sentinel*, July 2, 1948.

Historic Homes of Knoxville. "James White's Fort." hhknoxville.org, 2017.

James White's Fort. "The History of James White's Fort." jameswhitesfort.org, 2017.

Knoxville News Sentinel. "Chisholm Tavern Aged Knox Landmark Faces Demolition." May 5, 1948.

Larew, Mrs. Charles L. "Tavern's Past Offers Ample Grounds for Park Project." *Knoxville Journal*, June 20, 1945.

Patton, E.E. John. "John Chisholm Built First Tavern West of Smokies." *Knoxville Journal*, n.d.

Steely, Mike. "John Chisholm, Knoxville's Forgotten Scoundrel." *Knoxville Focus*, December 7, 2015.

WATE. "Why Is Knoxville a Frequent Test Market for Products and Restaurants?" wate.com, 2016.

Wheeler, Katherine. *The Tennessee Encyclopedia of History and Culture*. Nashville: Tennessee Historical Society, 1998.

Witt, Fanny Blow. "Captain John Chisholm." 1935.

CHAPTER 2

Bijou Theater. "History." knoxbijou.com, 2017.

Falconnier, John W. "Historic Old Lamar House, Over Century Old." *Knoxville Sentinel*, April 1, 1923.

Kelly, Dorothy E. "General Who? William P. Sanders." *Knoxville Civil War Round Table*, June 18, 2016.

Lamar, Gazaway Bugg. *Gazaway Bugg Lamar Papers*. Hargrett Rare Book and Manuscript Library, University of Georgia Libraries, 1798–1874.

Novelli, Dean. *The East Tennessee Historical Society's Publications* 56. Knoxville: East Tennessee Historical Society, 1984.

———. *The East Tennessee Historical Society's Publication* 57. Knoxville: East Tennessee Historical Society, 1985.

Patton, Charles V. "Old Records Reveal History of Knoxville's First Buildings." *Knoxville Journal*, September 23, 1945.

Sherman, William. "Memoirs of General W.T. Sherman 1863." sonofthesouth.net, 2017.

Templeton, Lucy Curtis. "Lamar House, First Archie Rhea's Tavern." *Knoxville News Sentinel*, July 22, 1945.

Thomas, Lois Reagan. "Bistro Closes; Buyer Reportedly Is Sought." January 12, 1989.

Weinstein, Max. Pagoda menu, 1934.

CHAPTER 3

Bond, Jesssie. "Pizza Place, Café Open Downtown." *Knoxville Journal*, August 11, 1990.

Branson, H.M. *Annual Hand Book of Knoxville*. Knoxville, TN: Tribune Job Office, 1892.

Brass, Larisa. "Knoxville Goes Wireless." *Knoxville News Sentinel*, July 20, 2003.

Brewer, Carson. "This Is Your Community." *Knoxville News Sentinel*, n.d.

Burdette, Shellie. "Macleod's Is a Knoxville Original." *Times Newspaper*, February 20, 2002.

Flannagan, Michael. "Hungry Workers." *Knoxville News Sentinel*, April 3, 2003.

Flory, Josh. "Kern Building Sold." *Knoxville News Sentinel*, October 20, 2010.

Harris, Roger. "Eatery Ladles Its Last Bowl." *Knoxville News Sentinel*, October 30, 2004.

Kephort, W.H. *Manufacturers of Knoxville*. Knoxville, TN: Bean, Warters & Co., 1901.

Knoxville Journal. "Kern's New Parlors." April 20, 1902.

———. "Soup Kitchen Creates Warm Feelings." October 1, 1987.

———. "The Soup Kitchen Now Offered as Franchise." October 16, 1986.

Knoxville News Sentinel. "Peter Kern Passed Away." October 28, 1907.

Morrison, Andrew. *Knoxville, Tennessee*. St. Louis, MO: Geo. W. Engelhardt, 1891.

Neal, Foree. "Designer Adds Polish to Blakely Hotel." *Knoxville News Sentinel*, April 18, 1990.

Neely, Jack. "The Accidental Knoxvillian." *Metro Pulse*, September 18, 1997.

———. "All You Can Eat, Pray, Love." *Metro Pulse*, September 2, 2010.

———. "May Notes." *Metro Pulse*, May 5, 2011.

———. "The Oliver's Twist." *Metro Pulse*, June 9, 2011.

———. "Questions of Identity." *Metro Pulse*, April 1, 2010.

———. "St. Oliver's Story." *Metro Pulse*, October 21, 2010.

Quiche N. Tell. "For Chilly Days Like These." *Knoxville Journal*, December 6, 1985.

White, Rick. "Blakely's Aims at 4 Star Status." *Knoxville News Sentinel*, September 22, 1990.

CHAPTER 4

Back in My Time. "Saloon Fare." backinmytime.blogspot.com, 2012.

Booker, Robert J. "Caldonia Fackler Johnson." *Tennessee Encyclopedia of History and Culture*. Nashville: Tennessee Historical Society, 1998.

———. "The History of Blacks in Knoxville, Tennessee." Beck Cultural Exchange Center, 1990.

Cournoyer, Shannon. "The Story of Knoxville's Cal Johnson." *Everything Knoxville*, July 1, 2009.

Erdoes, Richard. *Saloons of the Old West*. New York: Alfred A. Knopf, 1979.

Greene, Charles S. *Overland Monthly* and *Out West* magazines, December 1892.

Knoxville Heritage Quarterly. "Cal Johnson Building Rediscovered." Summer 1994.

Neely, Jack. "The Cal Johnson Building." *Knoxville Mercury*, January 14, 2016.

CHAPTER 5

Cristy, Kristi. "Family Lived Atop Father's Business." *Knoxville News Sentinel*, September 1, 1995.

Dean, Jerry. "Back in Business." *Knoxville News Sentinel*, July 4, 1999.

Durman, Louise. "The Patrick Sullivan Saloon." *Knoxville News Sentinel*, October 7, 1988.

Food Network. "Tim Love Bio." foodnetwork.com, 2017.

Harrington, Carly. "Historic Old City Venue Closes." *Knoxville News Sentinel*, August 16, 2011.

Henderson, Nancy Bearden. "Notorious and Proud of It." *New York Times*, Travel Section, February 21, 1999.

How, Eddie. "A Step Back in Time." *Knoxville Journal*, June 7, 1988.

Kimmons, Cherie. "Patrick Sullivan's Greets Diners." *Press Enterprise*, April 19, 1995.

Love, Tim. "About." cheftimlove.com, 2017.

Norman, Will. "Dine Well in an Historic Building." *Knoxville News Sentinel*, November 25, 1988.

Oppmann, Andrew. "Saloon, Shut Since 1907 to Reopen." *Knoxville News Sentinel*, January 14, 1988.

Trent, Kim. "Patrick Sullivan's Steakhouse & Saloon." *Knoxville Magazine*, June/July 2009.

Weiser, Kathy. "Old West Legends, Harvey Logan, aka Kidd Curry." legendsofamerica.com, 2014.

Chapter 6

Patton, Charles V. "Patton's Old Timer." *Knoxville Journal*, October 1, 1950.

Siegel/Bible. *Homecoming '86 for Siegel, Bible.* 1986.

The Vegetarian Cafeteria menu, 1922.

Chapter 7

Booker, Robert. "Knoxville Needed Hotels in Late 1800's." *Knoxville News Sentinel*, December 8, 2015.

Ennis, Rudy. "Bertha Walburn Clark, A Cultural Pioneer." www.knoxvillesymphony.com/our-history/bertha, 1984.

John. "333 W. Depot Street (Regas Square)—The Atkin Hotel." knoxvillelostandfound.blogspot.com, 2012.

Morrison, Andrew. *The City of Knoxville*, 1891.

Neely, Jack. "V for Vendome." *Metro Pulse*, January 28, 2010.

Trent, Kim. "The Vendome." *Knoxville Magazine*, August 2010.

Tumblin, J.C. "Knox Countians Who Made a Difference." fountaincityhistory.info, 2017.

Winegar, Mary Anna. "Strangers Within City's Gates." *Knoxville News Sentinel*, 1960.

"Yule Dinner at Schubert's." 1885.

Chapter 8

Hicks, Nannie Lee. "The History of Fountain City." April 23, 1956.

Knoxville News Sentinel. "In Early 1800's Fountain City." March 7, 1993.

Morrison, Andrew. *The City of Knoxville.* 1891.

Templeton, Lucy. "The Old Dummy Line." *Knoxville News Sentinel*, January 10, 1960.

Tumblin, Jim. "Emory Place and Central Market." *Farragut Shopper News*, April 8, 2013.

Veal, Kaye Franklin. "Annexation Didn't Destroy Fountain City." *Knoxville News Sentinel*, May 15, 1988.

Williams, Don. "There Were No Traffic Jams." *Knoxville News Sentinel*, March 7, 1993.

Winegar, Mary Anna. "Strangers within City's Gates." *Knoxville News Sentinel*, March 20, 1960.

CHAPTER 9

Browning, Robert M. "Damn the Torpedoes." *Naval History Magazine*, 2014.

History Channel. "David Farragut." history.com, 2017.

Hornberger, Matthew. "David Farragut America's First Admiral." National Park Service, 2012.

Hotel Monthly. "The Hotel Farragut of Knoxville, Tenn." N.d.

CHAPTER 10

Adallis, D. *History of Knoxville, TN Greek-American Colony 1904–1934.* Knoxville, TN: Knoxville Greek-American Colony & Friends, 1934.

Dean, Jerry. "End of an Eatery." *Knoxville News Sentinel*, April 4, 1999.

Durman, Louise. "Eating Ethnic Is Nothing New to Knoxville." *Knoxville News Sentinel*, July 31, 1977.

Fogarty, Martha. "Landmark Facelift Include Food." *Knoxville Journal*, May 4, 1977.

Hanshaw, Mark. "Different Era." *Knoxville News Sentinel*, March 29, 1985.

Madden, David. *Bijou.* New York: Crown Publishers, 1974.

McCarthy, Cormac. *Suttree.* New York: Random House, 1979.

Renshaw, Martha. "Gold Sun Spans 65 Year Tradition." *Knox County News*, September 23, 1971.

Weals, Vic. "Storekeeper T.E. Burns." *Knoxville Journal*, October 14, 1982.

CHAPTER 11

Adallis, D. *History of Knoxville, TN Greek-American Colony 1904–1934*. Knoxville, TN: Knoxville Greek-American Colony & Friends, 1934.

Balloch, Jim. "Raising a Glass to Regas." *Knoxville News Sentinel*, January 1, 2011.

Chamis, Eleni. "Grady's Parent Sells Eateries for $70 Million." *Knoxville News Sentinel*, November 3, 1995.

———. "Menu Change on Tap for Gay St. Brewery." *Knoxville News Sentinel*, June 19, 1996.

———. "Regas Has Lakeside Plans." *Knoxville News Sentinel*, August 18, 1996.

Davis, Marti. "Downtown Development Hindered." *Knoxville News Sentinel*, June 19, 1995.

Dining Out. "Charlie's Place, Regas on Seventeenth." *Knoxville News Sentinel*, August 15, 1981.

———. "Grady's." *Knoxville News Sentinel*, January 16, 1983.

The Doggie Bag. "What's in a Name." *Knoxville Journal*, December 11, 1981.

Durman, Louise. "At Regas They've Been Making Friends." *Knoxville News Sentinel*, July 3, 1994.

———. "Chef Comes to See First Grady's." *Knoxville News Sentinel*, June 28, 1995.

———. "Chef Shares His Own Brand of Taste." *Knoxville News Sentinel*, September 2, 1998.

———. "Heritage and New Ideas." *Knoxville News Sentinel*, December 19, 1982.

———. "The Old Is New Again at Regas." *Knoxville News Sentinel*, May 3, 2000.

———. "Pizza Oven and Rotisserie Are Main Ingredients." *Knoxville News Sentinel*, August 18, 1999.

Flannagan, Mike. "Regas Brothers Inc. Lifts Toast to Downtown." *Knoxville News Sentinel*, October 24, 2000.

———. "Regas Closing Gay Street Landmark." *Knoxville News Sentinel*, June 13, 2000.

———. "Regas to Reopen in Mid March." *Knoxville News Sentinel*, January 11, 2001.

Geisel, Amy. "A Different Twist." *Knoxville News Sentinel*, August 31, 1997.

———. "Regas Has New Restaurant." *Knoxville News Sentinel*, January 27, 1998.

Gunnels, Tom. "Wendy's Dave Thomas Fondly Remembered." *Knoxville News Sentinel*, January 31, 2007.

Jay, Aaron. "Past Presence." *Metro Pulse*, September 4, 1997.

Knoxville News Sentinel. "City Brew Closes Doors Downtown." July 11, 2001.

———. "Grady's Good Times, Restaurant, Lounge." August 1, 1982.

———. "Regas Bros. Café & Regas Coffee Shoppe." March 5, 1934.

———. "Second Generation Continues the Regas Tradition." July 3, 1994.

———. "Services Friday for Noted Restaurant Man." May 8, 1997.

———. "Wendy's to Open Knox Restaurant." August 6, 1975.

Lambert, Walter. "Brewhaha Tasty Ales, Savory Food." *Knoxville News Sentinel*, February 23, 2001.

McKinney, Melonee. "Founder of Wendy's Honored by Regas." *Knoxville News Sentinel*, June 8, 1994.

———. "Honesty Best Policy Wendy's Guru Says." *Knoxville News Sentinel*, December 2, 1994.

Neal, Suzanne. "Aubrey's to Make Service Highest Priority." *Knoxville News Sentinel*, February 12, 1992.

Nolan, Amy. "Friends Remember Wendy's Founder." *Knoxville News Sentinel*, January 9, 2007.

Silence, Michael. "Regas Square Honors Eatery." *Knoxville News Sentinel*, January 11, 2008.

Simmons, Laura. "New Owner Likes Grady's Just as It Is." *Knoxville News Sentinel*, January 11, 1989.

Taylor, Mallory. "The Gathering Place Regas the Restaurant." *City Limits*, May 1, 1986.

Wollenberg, Skip. "Wendy's Founder Finds Fame, Wants Sales." *Knoxville News Sentinel*, August 7, 1989.

Yeldell, Cynthia. "Grady's Closes Doors on Last Knox Diner." *Knoxville News Sentinel*, August 31, 2004.

CHAPTER 12

Barrett, Bob. "Hanging It Up? Noted Knoxville Restaurateur Sells." *Knoxville News Sentinel*, January 3, 1992.

Brinson, Charlie. "The History Behind Darryl's." *Eat It North Carolina*, January 12, 2011.

Constantine, Mary. "Smoky Smell of Success—UT Grad Parlays." *Knoxville News Sentinel*, May 27, 2012.

Darrylswoodfiredgrill.com.

Dining Out. "The Brass Rail." *Knoxville News Sentinel*, October 2, 1977.

———. "The Brass Rail." *Knoxville News Sentinel*, January 20, 1980.

———. "The Café de Roi." *Knoxville News Sentinel*, November 6, 1977.

———. "The Carriage House Restaurant." *Knoxville News Sentinel*, May 15, 1977.

The Doggie Bag. "Darryl's, Talk About Close Quarters." *Knoxville Journal*, April 28, 1983.

Durman, Louise. "Frank Kotsianas Realizes Dream." *Knoxville News Sentinel*, July 13, 1986.

———. "Fun, Food Blend at Darryl's." *Knoxville News Sentinel*, September 14, 1979.

———. "Kotsi's Charcoal Grill Is Going Caribbean." *Knoxville News Sentinel*, September 15, 1989.

———. "Kotsi's Comes to Franklin Square." *Knoxville News Sentinel*, September 5, 1986.

Fogarty, Martha. "Knoxville Restaurant Honored." *Knoxville Journal*, February 27, 1976.

———. "Restaurant Sold by George Consin." *Knoxville Journal*, January 13, 1977.

Knoxville Journal. "Brass Rail Being Constructed on Kingston Pike." 1978.

———. "The Brass Rail West." July 1, 1977.

———. "Carriage House." June 11, 1971.

———. "Nostalgia, Romance Spice Brass Rail West." March 24, 1977.

Knoxville News Sentinel. "Café de Roi International Cuisine." February 28, 1978.

———. "New Beautiful Garden Cafeteria." January 10, 1984.

Minor, Marty. "Darryl's Takes Care of Guests." *Knoxville News Sentinel*, July 4, 1984.

Reed, Vita. "Connor Buys Kotsi's Restaurant." *Knoxville News Sentinel*, December 7, 1991.

Renshaw, Martha. "Consin Has New Garden Cafeteria on Chapman." *Knoxville Journal*, October 24, 1980.

———. "Ivanhoe Restaurant Sold to Developers." *Knoxville News Sentinel*, March 5, 1975.

Thomas, Lois. "New Downtown Knoxville Location Sought." *Knoxville News Sentinel*, October 31, 1989.

Weirich, Frank. "The Ivanhoe, a Story of Hard Work and Success." *Knoxville News Sentinel*, January 28, 1968.

CHAPTER 13

Brewer, Carson. "With S&W Closed Slim Does Odd Jobs." *Knoxville News Sentinel*, 1981.

Citywide. "S&W Cafeteria a Downtown Landmark." *Citywide*, November 1994.

Dining Out. "S&W Cafeteria." *Knoxville News Sentinel*, April 13, 1980.

Flory, Josh. "Downtown Beautification Michigan Based Chain." *Knoxville News Sentinel*, June 19, 2011.

Gilbert, Bob. "Alcoa's Davis to Play for Tennessee State." *Knoxville News Sentinel*, August 23, 1998.

Julian, Harold. "Former S&W Employees Are Talking." *Knoxville News Sentinel*, August 13, 1989.

Kenner, Randy. "Longtime Waiter Slim Dickson Dies." *Knoxville News Sentinel*, August 20, 1998.

Knoxville Journal. "S&W to Open Here About April 1." February 3, 1927.

Knoxville News Sentinel. "Faces Reflect the Experience of Working for a Living." April 27, 1994.

Rebori, Stephen. "A Brief History of the S&W Cafeteria in Knoxville." February 1990.

Venable, Sam. "S&W Legend Play Return Engagement." *Knoxville News Sentinel*, October 6, 1987.

CHAPTER 14

Bean, Revonna. "Harold's Delicatessen." *East Tennessee Business Journal*, September 29, 1986.

Caruthers, Teree. "Kosher Cut Kindness." *Southern Living*, May 2000.

Constantine, Mary. "Knox Mason's Matt Gallaher." *Knoxville News Sentinel*, February 19, 2014.

Dean, Jerry. "50 Years Downtown." *Knoxville News Sentinel*, August 26, 1998.

Denk, Tom. "The Mystery Building Houses Harold's Deli." *Knoxville Journal*, March 24, 1986.

Harrington, Carly. "Harry's Deli to Close this Week." *Knoxville News Sentinel*, May 8, 2012.

———. "Harry's to Open in Old Harold's Site." *Knoxville News Sentinel*, October 15, 2010.

————. "New Management, Same Traditions." *Knoxville News Sentinel*, April 7, 2005.

Harris, Roger. "Harold's Ends Its 57 Year Tradition." *Knoxville News Sentinel*, July 8, 2005.

Kinnane, Beth. "Do It All Couple Cater to Enduring Appetites." *Knoxville Journal*, April 20, 1991.

Knoxville News Sentinel. "Co-owner of Harold's Deli Dies at 83." October 3, 2003.

Lee, Christie. "A Downtown Institution." *Knoxville Lifestyle*, July/August 1983.

Mallernee, Ellen. "Harold's Deli Locks Up." *Metro Pulse*, July 14, 2005.

Neely, Jack. "Addie Shersky: A Farewell to a Friend." *Metro Pulse*, October 9, 2003.

————. "Harold's Delicatessen." *Metro Pulse*, January 13, 1995.

————. "Harold's Forever." *Metro Pulse*, August 27, 1998.

————. "The Return of the Deli." *Metro Pulse*, October 14, 2010.

CHAPTER 15

Blackerby, Mike. "Memories of a Landmark." *Knoxville News Sentinel*, July 4, 2013.

County Chronicle. "Helma's a Star." July 29, 1985.

Durman, Louise. "Kress's Dish Was Mixture of Leftovers." *Knoxville News Sentinel*, February 10, 1993.

Flory, Josh. "High Rise Memories." *Knoxville News Sentinel*, December 26, 2007.

Knoxville News Sentinel. "Breakfast at Helma's." March 28, 1984.

————. "C.B. Alexander Wins First Courtesy Prize." August 17, 1952.

————. "First Anniversary Dixieland Drive-In." June 26, 1950.

————. "Inferno Drive-In Stirs Fond Memories." July 14, 2010.

————. "Knoxville Area Reverses U.S. Trend." March 27, 1955.

————. "Mrs. Gilreath Receives Restaurateur Award." October 2, 1977.

————. "Open House Terrace View Court." June 8, 1952.

Neely, Jack. "Silent and Waiting." *Metro Pulse*, November 13, 1997.

Weirich, Frank. "Truck Stop to Gourmet's Delight." *Knoxville News Sentinel*, April 6, 1966.

Williams, Don. "Friendships Form Over the Counter." *Knoxville News Sentinel*, March 5, 1993.

CHAPTER 16

Dean, Jerry. "Merchants on the Strip Say Face Lift Fuels." *Knoxville News Sentinel*, September 5, 1998.

Dining Out. "Hawkeye's Corner." *Knoxville News Sentinel*, December 6, 1981.

The Doggie Bag. "Could Have Been a Hardy Place." *Knoxville Journal*, July 15, 1982.

Durman, Louise. "Tom Is Cut from Hawkeye's Mold." *Knoxville News Sentinel*, April 11, 1984.

———. "Two Knoxville Restaurants Celebrate." *Knoxville News Sentinel*, September 2, 1988.

Harrington, Carly. "Old College Inn Is Out." *Knoxville News Sentinel*, May 18, 2011.

Knoxville News Sentinel. "Byerley's Sale Signals End of 30 Year Era." January 8, 1976.

———. "Ollie's Trolley." October 2, 1973.

Lakin, Matt. "Short Lived Streaking Drew National Attention." *Knoxville News Sentinel*, August 26, 2012.

Norman, Will. "The Falafel Hut Lives Up to Its Reputation." *Knoxville News Sentinel*, September 5, 1986.

Quiche N. Tell. "Quiche Trips Down Memory Lane." *Knoxville Journal*, May 2, 1986.

Schohl, Lisa. "Owner Sells Falafel Hut After 25 Years." *Knoxville News Sentinel*, September 1, 2007.

Simmons, Laura. "Longtime Strip Restaurateur." *Knoxville News Sentinel*, January 31, 1991.

Stanfield, Shannon. "The Strip's Appeal." *Knoxville News Sentinel*, August 27, 1999.

Steely, Mike. "Hawkeye's Denied Demolition." *Knoxville Focus*, June 20, 2016.

Venable, Sam. "Family Tradition Renewed." *Knoxville News Sentinel*, August 22, 1986.

Weintraub, Terri. "Proud Palestinians Give East Tennesseans." *Knoxville Journal*, 1989.

Yeldell, Cynthia. "Family Puts Falafel Hut on the Block." *Knoxville News Sentinel*, May 6, 2005.

CHAPTER 17

Aston-Wash, Barbara. "Old World Look Is Newly Arrived." *Knoxville News Sentinel,* July 16, 1976.

Bledsoe, Wayne. "Where Do You Want to Eat." *Knoxville News Sentinel,* May 29, 1988.

Constantine, Mary. "Smoky Smell of Success." *Knoxville News Sentinel,* May 27, 2012.

Cummins, Cynthia. "Local Art Dished Up." *Knoxville News Sentinel,* January 4, 1995.

Dining Out. "The Bahou." *Knoxville News Sentinel,* November 8, 1981.

————. "Half Shell House of Oyster and Beef." *Knoxville News Sentinel,* May 3, 1979.

————. "Jeremiah's." *Knoxville News Sentinel,* June 15, 1979.

————. "The Rathskeller." *Knoxville News Sentinel,* March 28, 1982.

The Doggie Bag. "Eggplant and Artichoke." *Knoxville Journal,* March 5, 1982.

————. "German Flavor Tops Rathskeller's List." *Knoxville Journal,* 1982.

Durman, Louise. "Bahou's Theme from Persian Rug." *Knoxville News Sentinel,* March 10, 1978.

————. "Local History Colors Jeremiah's Setting." *Knoxville News Sentinel,* September 22, 1977.

————. "70's Restaurateur Returns." *Knoxville News Sentinel,* August 6, 2003.

————. "Soup of the Day Black Beans." *Knoxville News Sentinel,* December 2, 1992.

Flanders, Sam. "Historic House Again to Be Site." *Knoxville News Sentinel,* August 1, 1990.

Flory, Josh. "Ali Baba Deli Closing After 4 Decades." *Knoxville News Sentinel,* March 2, 2013.

————. "Brewery Planned in Western Plaza." *Knoxville News Sentinel,* April 13, 2013.

————. "Building Rehab Reveals Long Forgotton Mural." *Knoxville News Sentinel,* August 4, 2007.

Hart, Anne. "New Restaurant, Retail for Pike Site." *Bearden Shopper News,* March 11, 2013.

Howard, Laffitte. "Vacant Home to Be Restored." *Knoxville News Sentinel,* August 6, 1977.

Jacobs, Don. "Half Shell Burns." *Knoxville Journal,* December 21, 1985.

James, Rebecca. "Knoxville Restaurant Plans Major Expansion." *East Tennessee Business Journal,* February 23, 1987.

Knoxville News Sentinel. "Kiva Grill Marks Its Grand Opening." December 2, 1992.

———. "Oyster and Beef House Will Open." July 20, 1975.

———. "Rathskeller to Reopen." January 9, 1982.

———. "Restaurant Opens in Baker-Peters House." June 9, 1993.

———. "Work to Begin on Half Shell." February 7, 1986.

Lambert, Walter. "Abner Would Probably Like This Attic." *Knoxville News Sentinel,* May 9, 1991.

———. "Half Shell Is Back Up to Standard." *Knoxville News Sentinel,* July 12, 1990.

———. "Painted Table Is Basic and Good." *Knoxville News Sentinel,* March 9, 1995.

———. "You'll Be Glad You Waited at Kiva Grill." *Knoxville News Sentinel,* August 13, 1992.

Lee, Victor. "Ali Baba's Is Dream Deli." *Knoxville News Sentinel,* March 29, 1981.

Loveday, Yvonne. "Strange Happenings Haunt Abner's Attic." *Knoxville News Sentinel,* October 30, 1991.

Lucke, Robby. "Knoxville Restaurant Offers Strange Menu." *East Tennessee Business Journal,* March 30, 1987.

Marcum, Ed. "Blackhorse Is at the Gate." *Knoxville News Sentinel,* August 1, 2015.

Neal, Suzanne. "At Anchor." *Knoxville News Sentinel,* September 16, 1987.

Norman, Will. "Skeller Brings on Nostalgia." *Knoxville News Sentinel,* October 16, 1987.

Quiche N. Tell. "Abner's Attic Features Tasty Southern." *Knoxville Journal,* August 22, 1991.

Reed, Vita. "Grill Catering to Southwest Taste." *Knoxville News Sentinel,* February 1, 1992.

Silence, Michael. "After the Fire." *Knoxville News Sentinel,* December 21, 1985.

Smith, Wendy. "Good Food, Family Sustain Ali Baba." *Bearden Shopper News,* 2013.

Vreeland, Eric. "Alderman Wants Baker Peters House." *Knoxville News Sentinel,* January 10, 1989.

CHAPTER 18

Bailey, Beecher. "Westside Dinner Theater Manager." *Knoxville Journal*, July 4, 1990.

Cain, Nancy. "Knox Dinner Theater Has Blount Connection." *Maryville Alcoa Times*, February 27, 1981.

Davis, Marti. "Movies to Share Billing with Food at Cinema Grill." *Knoxville News Sentinel*, September 1, 1999.

Hood, Lisa. "Riviera Closed Since 1976 May Become." *Knoxville News Sentinel*, November 7, 1980.

Knoxville Journal. "Renovated Riviera to Be Dinner Theater." February 17, 1981.

———. "Terrace Dinner Theater Readies for Opening." September 12, 1980.

Knoxville News Sentinel. "New Barn Theater Here Opens Dec. 1." November 20, 1966.

———. "New West Side Dinner Theater to Open." April 4, 1982.

———. "Terrace Theater Name Change." March 31, 1982.

———. "West Side Theater Closes Doors." May 2, 1983.

McKinney, Mary. "The Name's the Same." *Knoxville Journal*, May 5, 1982.

Norton, Debbie. "West Side Dinner Theatre Uniquely Different." *Knoxville Journal*, June 17, 1977.

Pickle, Betsy. "Raising the Curtain on the New Terrace Theater." *Knoxville News Sentinel*, 1982.

Shell, Malcolm. "The Old Barn Dinner Theater." *Shopper News*, December 16, 2013.

Sweeten, Tom. "Lights Shine Bright at Terrace." *Knoxville Journal*, October 18, 1980.

Weirich, Frank. "Barn Theater Is Filling, Entertaining." *Knoxville News Sentinel*, December 2, 1966.

———. "Fiddler to Open Dinner Theater on Wednesday." *Knoxville News Sentinel*, March 7, 1976.

CHAPTER 19

Aston-Wash, Barbara. "And the Graciousness Lingers On." *Knoxville News Sentinel*, August 8, 1977.

———. "Czar at the Nicholas." *Knoxville News Sentinel*, May 3, 1981.

———. "Now Where Is that Quonset Hut." *Knoxville News Sentinel*, February 23, 1984.

———. "The Orangery." *Knoxville News Sentinel*, September 1, 1986.

Carroll, Sheila. "Church Becomes Restaurant." *Daily Beacon*, October 4, 1979.

Catanoso, Justin. "Prime Suspect Held in Blaze." *Knoxville Journal*, April 25, 1985.

Dean, Jacquelyn. "Bye Old Club." *Knoxville News Sentinel*, March 26, 1992.

Dining Out. "Hanna's." *Knoxville News Sentinel*, August 28, 1977.

———. "The Orangery." *Knoxville News Sentinel*, December 1, 1977.

———. "The Orangery." *Knoxville News Sentinel*, September 2, 1979.

Durman, Louise. "Continental on the Mall." *Knoxville News Sentinel*, April 8, 1980.

———. "Dining au Continental." *Knoxville News Sentinel*, January 28, 1972.

———. "Tex Mex Adds to Mix Restaurateur Adds to His." *Knoxville News Sentinel*, December 19, 2001.

Flannagan, Michael. "Old City Ready for Change Wary Business." *Knoxville News Sentinel*, August 9, 2002.

Fogarty, Martha. "Orangery One of Top 25 Restaurants in US." *Knoxville News Sentinel*, December 9, 1975.

Geisel, Amy. "L'Hotel Designed with Visiting VIPs in Mind." *Knoxville News Sentinel*, February 14, 1990.

Glenn, Juanita. "Four Star Dining Gallery Lost in Orangery." *Knoxville Journal*, April 25, 1985.

Harrington, Carly. "The Orangery to Reopen." *Knoxville News Sentinel*, August 28, 2009.

Howard, Laffitte. "Orangery Owner to Open New Lord Lindsey." *Knoxville News Sentinel*, July 15, 1976.

Norris, Robert. "Classiness Speeds Demise of Fine Restaurants." *Knoxville News Sentinel*, June 9, 1981.

Robinson, Ronda. "Orangery's Segue." *Knoxville News Sentinel*, March 29, 2009.

———. "Revered Developer Kendrick Dies." *Knoxville News Sentinel*, May 4, 2009.

Thomas, Lois. "Fire Guts Orangery Building." *Knoxville News Sentinel*, April 24, 1985.

CHAPTER 20

Bacon, Susan. "The Environment: Tropical Treat." *Knoxville Journal*, July 8, 1977.

Dining Out. "The Environment." *Knoxville News Sentinel*, July 17, 1977.

———. "The Environment." *Knoxville News Sentinel*, September 12, 1982.

Durman, Louise. "Feeding People at the Zoo." *Knoxville News Sentinel*, July 22, 1982.

Knoxville News Sentinel. "Growing Zoo Adding Pleasant Dining." May 17, 1977.

———. "July 3 Opening Planned for Restaurant at Zoo." June 25, 1977.

McKinney, Mary. "New Summer Menu at the Environment." *Knoxville Journal*, June 29, 1978.

Weirich, Frank. "The Environment." *Knoxville News Sentinel*, December 2, 1977.

CHAPTER 21

Dean, Jerry. "Marina Taking Shape." *Knoxville News Sentinel*, May 24, 1998.

The Doggie Bag. "A Family Restaurant Where the Parents Eat in Peace." *Knoxville Journal*, September 25, 1981.

———. "With Time Cajun's Will Corner Consistency." *Knoxville Journal*, April 9, 1982.

Durman, Louise. "Fisherman Serves Fun Too." *Knoxville News Sentinel*, October 25, 1978.

———. "New Restaurant on River Will Kick Off." *Knoxville News Sentinel*, July 2, 2000.

———. "Restaurateur Details Game Plan for Success." *Knoxville News Sentinel*, August 29, 2001.

Hetherington, Bob. "Officials Hope to Clear Questions." *Knoxville News Sentinel*, July 2, 1978.

Knoxville News Sentinel. "Cajun's Wharf Ordered to Replace Wiring." February 5, 1982.

———. "Cars Towed from Lot Near Cajun's Wharf." August 19, 1982.

———. "Duct Tumbles at Restaurant." February 5, 1982.

———. "Has Anyone Ever Met the Real Buster Muggs." February 25, 1983.

———. "Landing a Restaurant." July 21, 1981.

———. "Real Seafood Co. Sold for $400,000." September 18, 1987.

———. "Restaurant to be Built on Baum's Pond Site." June 19, 1977.

———. "Waterfront Grill Delivers Lofty Views." April 13, 2007.

Lambert, Walter. "The View Is Fine the Food's Divine." *Knoxville News Sentinel*, October 20, 2000.

Moulton, John. "TVA Challenges Parking Spaces at Cajun's." *Knoxville News Sentinel*, December 4, 1981.

Yeldell, Cynthia. "Boathouse Back in Business." *Knoxville News Sentinel*, November 10, 2006.

Chapter 22

Anderson, Christine. "Have Label Did Travel to WF." *Knoxville News Sentinel*, April 25, 1982.

Brewer, Carson. "Sunsphere Proposed as Expo Theme." *Knoxville News Sentinel*, March 16, 1980.

Durman, Louise. "Best Eatin' Up and Down." *Knoxville News Sentinel*, February 28, 1982.

———. "Restaurant Menus Services to Grow." *Knoxville News Sentinel*, November 24, 1982.

Franich, Frank. *The 1982 World's Fair Official Guidebook*. Knoxville, TN: Exposition Publishers, 1982.

Knoxville News Sentinel. "Chronology for World's Fair Issues." April 28, 2002.

———. "Hardee's Leaving Sunsphere." March 28, 1984.

Roark, Courtney. "Sunsphere an Iconic Structure." *Greater Knoxville Business Journal*, March 2017.

Veal, Kaye. "Sunsphere to Relax, Emphasize Fine Dining." *Knoxville News Sentinel*, November 24, 1982.

Chapter 23

Aston-Wash, Barbara. "Candy Factory to Serve Worldly Foods." *Knoxville News Sentinel*, October 11, 1981.

Bledsoe, Wayne. "Food, Music Return to Strohaus." *Knoxville News Sentinel*, August 16, 1990.

Brown, Fred. "Candy Maker Brings Sweet History Full Circle." *Knoxville News Sentinel*, January 14, 1996.

Cottin, Lynn. "Fair Fare." *Knoxville Lifestyle,* July 1982.

Durman, Louise. "Taste Mexican Difference." *Knoxville News Sentinel,* January 19, 1983.

Franich, Frank. *The 1982 World's Fair Official Guidebook.* Knoxville, TN: Exposition Publishers, 1982.

Glenn, Juanita. "Fair's Long Gone but Strohaus." *Knoxville Journal,* November 5, 1982.

Kirkpatrick, William. "Foundry Forges Ahead." *Volunteer Valley Business Journal,* May 17, 1999.

Knoxville News Sentinel. "Candy Firm Is 41 Years Old." September 15, 1929.

———. "Concession Stands." May 2, 1982.

———. "Retired Candy Maker Arthur H. Steere Dies." April 2, 1962.

———. "Skinny Dippers." May 2, 1982.

Morris, Betsy. "The Strohaus Changes the Foundry's Tune." *Knoxville News Sentinel,* May 23, 1982.

Siler, Charles. "Festhaus May Stay After Fair." *Knoxville News Sentinel,* December 11, 1987.

Thorpe, Steven. "Korea Hexagon and a Trip." *Knoxville News Sentinel,* May 2, 1982.

Toplovich, Ann. "1982 World's Fair Highlights Historic Preservation." *Courier,* 1982.

CHAPTER 24

Chamis, Eleni. "Southbound at the L&N." *Knoxville News Sentinel,* August 28, 1996.

Dean, Jacquelyn. "L&N Grill Now Closed." *Knoxville News Sentinel,* October 12, 1993.

Dining Out. "L&N Fish Market." *Knoxville News Sentinel,* May 2, 1982.

Durman, Louise. "An Interlude with Pierre." *Knoxville News Sentinel,* February 5, 1982.

———. "Jockey Club Brings Fine Dining." *Knoxville News Sentinel,* March 1, 2000.

Siler, Charles. "Fish Market to Offer Fresh Seafood." *Knoxville News Sentinel,* November 1, 1981.

Warnick, Marta. "Grill It Yourself Steak." *Knoxville News Sentinel,* October 28, 1982.

Chapter 25

Chamis, Eleni. "Lucille's in Old City Closing." *Knoxville News Sentinel*, October 24, 1996.

Fields, Linda. "Annie's Opens to Rave Reviews." *Knoxville News Sentinel*, July 27, 1983.

Geisel, Amy. "Annie's Restaurant Old City Landmark Closes." *Knoxville News Sentinel*, August 22, 1989.

Harrington, Carly. "Old City Jazz Club Changing Its Tune." *Knoxville News Sentinel*, June 23, 2004.

Jones, Tracy. "How Kristopher Kendrick's Preservationist Vision." *Knoxville Mercury*, October 12, 2016.

Knoxville Magazine. "Missing Annie's...A Very Special Restaurant." September 2008.

Norman, Will. "Annie's Is Indeed Very Special." *Knoxville News Sentinel*, October 3, 1986.

Oppmann, Andrew. "Parking Troubles Hurt." *Knoxville News Sentinel*, January 5, 1988.

Veal, Kaye. "Annie's to Become Lucille's." *Knoxville News Sentinel*, September 16, 1989.

Chapter 26

Constantine, Mary. "T. Ho Bistro to Close." *Knoxville News Sentinel*, September 1, 2007.

Harrington, Carly. "On a Roll." *Knoxville News Sentinel*, March 5, 2008.

Kaczka, Lisette. "T. Ho Bistro." *Knoxville News Sentinel*, February 8, 2006.

Lambert, Walter. "Unforgettable Egg Rolls Launch Fine Meal." *Knoxville News Sentinel*, August 7, 1997.

Marcum, Ed. "Pint House." *Knoxville News Sentinel*, October 4, 2006.

Park, Pam. "An American Success." *Knoxville News Sentinel*, April 30, 1997.

Perkins, Dennis. "Umami Revival." *Knoxville Mercury*, May 26, 2016.

Simmons, Morgan. "Thanh Ho Family Brings Delicacies." *Knoxville Journal*, 1987.

CHAPTER 27

Cummins, Cynthia. "Restaurateur to Jazz Up Oriental Food." *Knoxville News Sentinel*, September 15, 1993.

Durman, Louise. "Cha Cha: Where a Little Means a Lot." *Knoxville News Sentinel*, November 7, 2001.

———. "Local Diners Can Expect Feel Good Growth." *Knoxville News Sentinel*, January 2, 2002.

Harrington, Carly. "Hard Times to Close Cha Cha's Doors." *Knoxville News Sentinel*, December 4, 2007.

Lambert, Walter. "Revel in Mango's Delectable Whimsy." *Knoxville News Sentinel*, December 8, 2000.

———. "Tap into Tasty Tapas at Cha Cha." *Knoxville News Sentinel*, November 28, 2001.

Metro Pulse. "Mango." Restaurant Guide, Fall 1999.

Mitchell, Bryan. "Owner of 5 Eateries Dies on S.C. Trip." *Knoxville News Sentinel*, May 16, 2004.

Nelson, Kristi. "Signature Cocktails." *Knoxville News Sentinel*, June 24, 2003.

Yeldell, Cynthia. "Kin to Run Restaurants of Man Who Drowned." *Knoxville News Sentinel*, May 22, 2004.

———. "One Siao Restaurant Shuttered." *Knoxville News Sentinel*, January 27, 2006.

———. "Restaurant Exec Gets Cha Cha." *Knoxville News Sentinel*, December 31, 2004.

———. "Siaos Looking Ahead." *Knoxville News Sentinel*, June 15, 2004.

CHAPTER 28

Barker, Scott. "Rebirth of Market Square Starts at Shovel Level." *Knoxville News Sentinel*, November 8, 2002.

———. "Revamp of Market Square Cleared to Start." *Knoxville News Sentinel*, August 24, 2002.

Bond, Jessie. "Pizza Place, Café Open Downtown." *Knoxville Journal*, August 11, 1990.

Brass, Larisa. "Downtown Restaurant Lula to Close Saturday." *Knoxville News Sentinel*, September 29, 2000.

Dean, Jerry. "Market Square Gets Mexican Eatery." *Knoxville News Sentinel*, April 23, 1998.

———. "Tomato Head Temporarily Closed." *Knoxville News Sentinel*, February 23, 2000.

Durman, Louise. "Fruit to Nuts Desserts Worth Celebrating." *Knoxville News Sentinel*, November 25, 1998.

———. "Mahasti Makes Mark on Market." *Knoxville News Sentinel*, April 21, 1999.

———. "Tempers Flare but Good Taste Prevails." *Knoxville News Sentinel*, September 8, 1999.

Eva Magazine. "Mahasti Vafaie, the Tomato Head." November 2007.

Harrington, Carly. "Leading with Her Heart." *Greater Knoxville Business Journal*, August 2010.

Harris, Chandra. "Market Square's Women Shake Off the Dust." *Knoxville News Sentinel*, August 10, 2003.

Lambert, Walter. "Lula Strives to Be Southwestern and Succeeds." *Knoxville News Sentinel*, April 23, 1999.

Marcum, Ed. "When Chris Whittle Could Do No Wrong." *Knoxville News Sentinel*, 2012.

Vines, Georgiana. "Redevelopment Plan Would Help Business." *Knoxville News Sentinel*, October 3, 2000.

CHAPTER 29

Durman, Louise. "New Flavors Enhance the Plain Old Potato." *Knoxville News Sentinel*, January 29, 1997.

———. "A Palette of Potatoes." *Knoxville News Sentinel*, February 2, 2000.

———. "Restaurants Favorites." *Knoxville News Sentinel*, March 20, 1996.

Flannagan, Michael. "Reviving Market Square." *Knoxville News Sentinel*, June 21, 2002.

Knoxville News Sentinel. "In Brief." November 5, 2003.

———. "Knoxville Café, Consulting Firm Get National Nods." April 25, 1999.

Marcum, Ed. "Downtown Café Finds New Home." *Knoxville News Sentinel*, September 18, 2002.

Vines, Georgiana. "Still Serving." *Knoxville News Sentinel*, July 7, 2013.

Chapter 30

Comer, M.E. "Latin Flare." *Knoxville Magazine*, 2007.

Dinanath, Janelle. "Bite This." *Eva Magazine*, April 2008.

Harrington, Carly. "La Costa Owner Sells Eatery to Focus." *Knoxville News Sentinel*, October 16, 2008.

————. "La Costa's Green Ways." *Knoxville News Sentinel*, November 8, 2007.

Knoxville News Sentinel. "Eatery on Tap at Broadway and Jackson." September 21, 2011.

Latham, Katherine. "TextMe." *Knoxville News Sentinel*, May 15, 2007.

ABOUT THE AUTHOR

East Tennessee native Paula Johnson has made herself an expert in Knoxville history, haute cuisine, hole-in-the-wall eateries and hidden culinary hot spots. Since creating Knoxville Food Tours in 2010, Paula has personally led over eight hundred food tours and has also served as a step-on guide for bus groups touring Knoxville and the surrounding area. In 2016, she was asked to partner with the University of Tennessee's Personal Development Food and Wine Courses and also with WDVX's *Tennessee Farm Table* radio program. In 2017, Knoxville Food Tours received the Service Supplier of the Year Award from the Greater Knoxville Hospitality Association.